DATE DUE

#47-0108 Peel Off Pressure Sensitive

Lou Henry Hoover: Essays on a Busy Life

Edited by
Dale C. Mayer

Lou Henry Hoover

ESSAYS ON A BUSY LIFE

High Plains
Publishing
Company

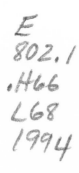

Library of Congress Catalog Card Number 93-78297
ISBN 1-881019-04-7

Photographs courtesy of the Herbert Hoover
Presidential Library, West Branch, Iowa.

High Plains Publishing Company, Inc.
Post Office Box 1860
Worland, Wyoming 82401

To the Questers of Iowa

whose generous grant made this publication possible and whose continuing support for the Hoover Library is gratefully appreciated.

Contents ✺

Lou Henry Hoover ✠
A Chronological Summary

1874 Born in Waterloo, Iowa, on March 29 to Charles D. and Florence Weed Henry.

1887 Henry family moves to Whittier, California staying three years before moving to Monterey in 1890.

1894 Meets Herbert Hoover in a geology laboratory at Stanford University.

1898 Receives degree in geology from Stanford University. Accepts position as secretary-treasurer of Monterey chapter of the American Red Cross, her first known service in a public service organization.

1899 Marries Herbert Hoover at her parents' home in Monterey on February 10. Their honeymoon takes place on a steamer enroute to Hoover's new position in China. Mrs. Hoover studies Chinese and begins a collection of porcelains and material for a projected book on China.

1900 Boxer Rebellion breaks out in China. Hoovers are trapped with 800 Europeans and a few Americans in Tientsin. Begins, but does not finish, a book on their seige experience.

1900-09   Travels around the world several times with her husband and her sons. Visits Italy, Egypt, India, Australia, New Zealand, Burma, Japan, China, and Russia.

1907-14   Collaborates with her husband in the translation of De Re *Metallica*, a 16th century mining book written in Latin. The Hoovers are awarded a gold medal in 1914 by the Mining and Metallurgical Society of America for their achievement.

1909-12   London periodicals publish her biographical essays on the dowager Empress of China and British seismologist John Milne.

1914-16   As president of the Society of American Women in London at the outbreak of World War I, she mobilizes the Society to help repatriate American tourists stranded in Europe. Presides over Society's expanded relief programs until her return to the U.S. in 1917. Also raises funds for Belgian relief.

1917-19   Hoovers return to Washington, D.C. She becomes a Girl Scout national commissioner and leader of Troop 8. Organizes and subsidizes the operation of a club and residence for young women who are employed by the Food Administration. Also helps to organize the American Red Cross' efforts to return wounded American soldiers to their homes.

1921   Drives her car from California to Washington, D.C. after her mother's funeral. Visits Waterloo and West Branch enroute.

1922   Helps to found the National Amateur Athletic Federation and serves as president of the Women's Division of the NAAF until its merger with a similar organization in 1940.

1922-25   Tours country as president of the Girl Scouts of America. Is a very popular speaker at local and regional meetings.

1924   Heads National Women's Conference on Law Enforcement in response to the Teapot Dome scandals.

1925-29   Vice President of the Girl Scouts and chairman of the national board of commissioners (1925-28). She becomes Honorary President during the Hoover Administration, 1929-33.

1928-29   Takes a limited part in the campaign of 1928. After her husband's election, she accompanies him on a good-will tour of Latin America. Herbert Hoover is inaugurated on March 4, 1929.

1929   Breaks White House racial barrier by entertaining the wife of Oscar DePriest, a black congressman from Chicago.

1929-33   She and her secretaries conduct extensive research on the history, traditions, and furnishings of the White House. Purchases exact reproductions of Monroe era furnishings for the White House permanent collections.

       Conducts confidential, personal relief program to provide assistance for needy families during the Depression.

1933-44   Assumes leadership role in Pro America, the California League of Women Voters and in Republican Women's activities nationally and in the state of California. Helps to promote sales of her husband's books: *American's First Crusade* and *The Problems of Lasting Peace* in 1941-42.

       Becomes progressively more involved in activities of the Salvation Army as an organizer of fund raising dinners and bazaars and as a western regional officer.

       At the onset of World War II, she helps her husband to mobilize relief for Finland, Poland, Belgium and several other small democracies overrun by the Nazis.

1937   Collaborates with Elizabeth Sprague Coolidge to found the Friends of Music at Stanford. Also an active supporter of numerous campus organizations at Stanford University and musical and artistic organizations in the San Francisco area.

1944   Dies in New York at her Waldorf Astoria apartment on January 7.

Foreword ✨

A volume of essays about the life and work of Lou Henry Hoover is a very welcome addition to the growing historical literature about first ladies in the twentieth century. Among the seventeen women who have occupied the position since Theodore Roosevelt took office in 1901, Lou Henry Hoover is probably the first lady about whom the least is known. As the essays in this book make clear, Mrs. Hoover deserves to be more widely recognized both for her achievements before and after the White House years and for the contributions she made during the time when her husband was president. Few first ladies have had more interesting and varied lives or have affected institutions relating to American women more directly than Lou Henry Hoover.

The range of talents that Mrs. Hoover possessed is striking. She was an athlete, scientist, linguist, historian, and gifted organizer. From her days on the Stanford University campus until she lived in the White House, she found creative ways to promote a greater awareness of what women could do. She showed her abilities early in the women's clubs to which she belonged. Lou Hoover is a superb example of the importance of voluntary associations in American women's history.

During the 1920s, Mrs. Hoover was a guiding spirit of the Girl Scouts, an organization whose significance in shaping the attitudes and values of young girls in the United States is only just beginning to receive its due recognition. This book demonstrates that abundant materials about the Girl Scouts await researchers at the Herbert Hoover Presidential Library. Mrs. Hoover's records offer almost a month-by-month record of how Girl Scout leaders made decisions and developed policy.

Equally important was Mrs. Hoover's work to encourage athletics among women during the 1920s. The National Amateur Athletic Federation and its Women's Division, with which Mrs. Hoover was so involved, represent a clear continuity with the efforts over the past twenty years to enhance equity in college athletics among men and women. Exploration of what Mrs. Hoover did, the issues she confronted, and the obstacles she encountered will reveal important precedents for modern proponents of enhanced opportunities for women in sports. A national network of women sports advocates existed during this period, most of whom have now been largely forgotten. Yet there were connections between Mrs. Hoover and a figure such as Anna Hiss at the University of Texas, another advocate of womens sports during these years. One of Hiss's students at the time Mrs. Hoover was first lady was Claudia Alta Taylor, more widely known now as Lady Bird Johnson.

Mrs. Hoover's years as first lady have often been treated as simply a prelude to the more exciting activism and liberal commitments of Eleanor Roosevelt. What the Hoover papers reveal, however, is a woman whose political views were in line with her husband's blend of progressive procedural reform and conservative economic policy, but whose disposition and energy led her to activism in the pursuit of her goals.

In the White House, Lou Hoover was a very visible public figure who gave radio addresses to the nation (the first first lady to do so), performed numerous ceremonial duties, and used her influence to support her husband's relief programs. During the Depression, she mobilized the Girl Scouts to provide voluntary relief assistance to Americans confronted with economic want. In the process, she entered the political and policy process more fully than had any first lady before her. The result was a program that provided an example of what a presidential wife could accomplish despite the constraints of her position and the times in which she lived.

The study of first ladies is moving from the earlier reliance on memoirs and readily available published sources to an intensive exploration of the rich documentation available at presidential libraries about these women. No woman better illustrates the possibilities of that approach than does Lou Hoover. The chapters of this book indicate what awaits the careful and thoughtful student of Lou Hoover's life in her papers. Perhaps the essays will encourage a scholar to begin writing the much-needed comprehensive biography of this fascinating woman. At the very least, this book will introduce modern readers to a woman of multiple talents and diverse accomplishments, who had as her husband once remarked, the "tender affection of an indomitable soul."

LEWIS L. GOULD

Mrs. Hoover's love of the outdoors provided the focus for many of her activities. The busy First Lady especially enjoyed horseback riding in the rugged terrain surrounding Camp Rapidan.

Introduction ❧ A Quick Review of a Busy Life

Dale C. Mayer

The opening of the Lou Henry Hoover Papers in 1985 was greeted with considerable enthusiasm by researchers and the public. Researchers who have used the papers since then have registered considerable surprise over the wide range of Mrs. Hoover's interests and activities.

Widely traveled, she had circled the globe several times before 1910 with her husband and two young sons. Languages fascinated her and it was reputed that she could carry on conversations in Chinese, French, and several other languages. On inspection trips with her husband she often went down into the mines, much to the consternation of superstitious Chinese miners. Equally at home in a primitive camp or a Victorian drawing room, she could plan a diplomatic reception for five hundred guests or stalk and shoot wild game with equal aplomb. She was also a serious scholar who researched the gold-mining techniques of the Egyptians, wrote articles on the lives of a noted British seismologist and the Chinese empress, and translated an obscure mining textbook from Latin into English.

Her public service endeavors were equally as diverse and no less interesting. Apparently her first position in a public service organization was with the American Red Cross. During the summer of 1898 she had been recruited by her mother to help roll bandages for men wounded in the Spanish-American War and soon found herself serving as secretary-treasurer of the local chapter.

During World War I, she was president of the American Women's War Relief Fund in London, promoted the sale of Belgian lace to support the Commission for Relief in Belgium, and organized a social club for young women who had come to Washington to work in the U.S. Food Administration.

Between 1918 and her death in 1944 she became one of the more important leaders in the Girl Scout movement, helped set up the Red Cross Canteen Escort Service for wounded servicemen returning from the war, became the driving force behind the establishment of the National Amateur Athletic Federation, ran her own informal relief organization during the Depression, was one of the founders of the Friends of Music at Stanford University, and also gave liberally of her time and energies to the western region of the Salvation Army. She also lent her name to and made appearances on behalf of several dozen other organizations.

Although it is hard to imagine why this former first lady (who charmed everyone who ever met her) is not better known, there is a simple explanation. The Hoovers, unlike present-day celebrities, did not seek public adulation and the former president directed that Mrs. Hoover's papers should remain closed for a period of twenty years after his death. The only biography of Lou Hoover is long out of print, but researchers who have become acquainted with her are determined to place her in the ranks of America's most notable women. In the meantime, this volume is offered as a preview of things to come.

When they begin their investigations, researchers are particularly pleased to discover that the Lou Henry Hoover Papers provide a fair amount of information about the early years of her life. (The earliest item in the collection is, appropriately, a gushing letter from Lou's grandmother Weed who had just returned from seeing the new baby.)

Rosemary Carroll makes good use of these early materials in an exploration of Lou's formative years that documents the development of the leadership traits that Mrs. Hoover so frequently displayed as an adult. Carroll's essay takes us up to 1917, the year the Hoovers returned to the United States after Mr. Hoover's appointment as U.S. Food Administrator. The story begins, however, in 1874 in Waterloo, Iowa.

Several coincidences may be noted in the early lives of Lou and Herbert Hoover. Born approximately six months and about 100 miles apart, they shared a love of nature and outdoor recreation. Both left the state at about the same point in their lives under difficult circumstances. The orphaned Bert was separated from his brother and sister and sent to live with relatives in Oregon. Lou's mother suffered from asthma so the family was forced to move to a more hospitable climate in California. Having left Iowa in 1884, both Lou and Herbert spent an important part of their adolescence in California and eventually wound up at Stanford University as contemporaries.

It was a shared interest in geology that had brought them to Stanford and led to their first meeting. Years later, in his memoirs, Herbert would recall his delight when he realized that he had actually met a young lady who would want to share the nomadic life of a mining engineer. Their marriage was delayed until he had established himself as a successful mining engineer, but their relationship was sustained through long absences by a common interest in the outdoors and geology.

It is easy to see how Lou's early introduction to the joys of camping and hiking not only prepared her for the nomadic life as the wife of a mining engineer but actually whetted an appetite for travel and adventure. In commenting on her new son-in-law, Lou's mother observed that Lou had welcomed the chance to live in China and that the proposed peripatetic, globe-trotting life seemed "her ideal."[1] After their marriage in 1899, the Hoovers spent their honeymoon on a steamer enroute to China and Bert's new duties as chief mining consultant to the Chinese government. For the next fourteen years the family was based in London while Mrs. Hoover and her two young sons accompanied her husband to exotic locations in Egypt, India, Burma, Australia, China, Japan and Russia.

By 1912, although they did not then realize it, the Hoovers' days of travel were nearly over. Herbert Hoover had risen to the top of his profession, and having concluded that making large sums of money was no trick, he had begun looking for new challenges and outlets for his energies. The thought of public service crossed his mind several times. When World War I broke out in the fall of 1914, the Hoovers were asked to organize an American Committee to aid stranded American travelers who had been caught in the early confusion and chaos of the war.

Because most of the available steamship berths had already been booked for the tourist season and return to the United States was likely to be delayed, Lou and her friends in the Society of American Women in London enlarged the scope of their activities to cope with the long-term problems of the stranded. Over the next five years, the Society expanded its activities until it was running woolen mills and field dressing stations and hospitals for the benefit of Allied soldiers. The Society also established a maternity hospital in Belgium and nurseries in northern France.

Christmas 1914 brought a grim reality. Unless the Belgians received large quantities of food immediately, the eight million people of the tiny nation were going to starve. In peacetime, Belgians depended on exports for 65 percent of their food. Having been overrun by the German army in the first weeks of the war, the Belgians found themselves behind German lines and subject to a British blockade. Everyone looked to the United States, as the most important neutral nation, for leadership in meeting Belgium's need. When the American ambassador in London, Walter Hines Page, was ordered to find an American to head up the relief effort, he immediately thought of Herbert Hoover.

Hoover's two most difficult challenges were to secure the cooperation of the British and German high commands and to consolidate several enthusiastic American groups into a unified relief commission. Lou returned to the United States in 1915 and made several speeches on behalf of the Commission for Relief in Belgium, but most of her energies were channeled into the ever-expanding programs of the American Women's War Relief Fund. When Herbert Hoover was appointed U.S. Food Administrator in 1917, the Hoovers returned to the United States and Lou's public service interests immediately took on new dimensions.

The primary objective of the Food Administration was to encourage Americans to conserve sugar, fats, meat, flour, and other important staples so that America could feed its allies. Although the Food Administration conducted research and developed recipes that were aimed at introducing new foods to American tables, it was most visible through a well-orchestrated publicity campaign that promoted "meatless days" and "wheatless days" through a constant barrage of posters and slogans. These food conservation measures soon became known, collectively, as "Hooverizing."

A minor scandal was narrowly avoided when one Washington woman complained in the press that the Hoovers were not practicing what the Food Administration preached. An elaborate rebuttal, which appeared in the pages of the *Ladies' Home Journal*, pointed out that Mrs. Hoover's conservation measures were much more stringent than those advocated by the Food Administration. In fact, "what she saw and what she learned in Europe led Mrs. Hoover to place her . . . home on a food conservation basis" several months before the Food Administration campaigns began.[2]

It is apparent from her speech and clipping files that Lou took an active interest in the Food Administration's experiments with new cereal grains and in the recipes that came out of its test kitchens. Although she rarely delivered a formal speech, her files indicate that she made many appearances at which she made informal remarks promoting the use of new staple grains and other conservation measures. During this period, from 1917 to 1919, she was also involved in other war-related public service activities.

One of these stemmed directly from her interest in the Food Administration and her apparent feeling that her husband's organization should be one big, happy family. Noticing that the War had brought a lot of young women to Washington to work as secretaries, she immediately became aware of their difficulties in finding suitable places to live. The federal government had built several temporary office buildings and the housing situation had become especially acute.

Lou's response was to organize the Food Administration Women's Club. Headquartered in a large house that she rented and then equipped with a large kitchen, the club combined many of the practical features of a boarding house with the social programs of a college sorority.

Toward the end of the war, the Food Administration was disbanded and Lou's interests turned to America's wounded servicemen. In 1918 she became one of the planners who helped the American Red Cross to establish the Canteen Escort Service. This organization functioned briefly at the war's end to provide escorts who would meet hospital ships and make wounded servicemen comfortable on the trains taking them home.

When peace finally came late in 1918, Lou turned to other activities. If anything, she would be equally busy in the 1920s as she had been during the war. She was just beginning her Girl Scout work and would soon become heavily involved in the founding of the National Amateur Athletic Federation (NAAF) and the development of women's athletics. How Lou came to play a vital role in the development of these organizations is detailed in chapters by Rebecca Christian and Jan Beran.

The emphasis on active, outdoor programs was common to both the Girl Scouts and NAAF. In retrospect, this emphasis was undoubtedly one of the main reasons for the tremendous growth of Girl Scouting during the years when Mrs. Hoover was involved in shaping the agenda of the Girl Scouts. The camping and hiking programs were her favorites and she seldom missed an opportunity to remind leaders of their importance.

A basic assumption underlying the Girl Scout program was the importance of exploring and learning under the guidance and encouragement of enthusiastic adults. Mrs. Hoover's speeches at leadership conferences and workshops constantly repeated the theme that girls could learn to do anything and should be encouraged to pursue interests that attracted them. This prepared them to be good citizens, mothers, and homemakers. Implicit in this preparation was the assumption that the future of the country depended on producing well-educated and informed citizens who would be willing to contribute to the well-being of the communities in which they lived. A major goal of Girl Scouting was to prepare each girl for her all-important role as a shaper of yet another generation—as a mother and a homemaker.

During the period of Mrs. Hoover's service on the board the Girl Scout movement expanded dramatically from just under 168,000 members in 1927—the year of Juliette Low's death—until it reached over 1,035,000 members in 1944. There were many reasons for this phenomenal success.

The outdoor camping program was a relatively novel feature in the 1920s and the money Lou raised—almost single-handedly—was wisely spent on expanding the camping program and on leadership training and on an attractive national magazine which helped to tie the movement together. Another factor that should not be overlooked was the democratic leadership philosophy that local troop leaders were urged to adopt. Lou often spoke of the importance of "leading from the back"; being available to provide encouragement and assistance, but carefully avoiding too much direction that might inhibit the girls' curiosity as they discovered the world for themselves.

A better understanding of the apparent success of Girl Scouting in these formative years would be very beneficial. It would not only allow both scholars and the general public to evaluate Lou

7

Hoover's contributions and impact but also, and more importantly, we could profit from a discussion of the goals and methods employed by the Girl Scouts during the early years of its existence in seeking to shape an agenda for child welfare organizations in its day. It would also be interesting to see whether local leaders have continued to heed Lou's advice to "lead from the back."

Viewed from the perspective of a later generation her comments at leadership conferences raise several interesting questions about her attitudes on the place of young girls and women in society and her own place in women's history. There is an intriguing tension between her repeated statements that girls should be encouraged to seek out and pursue their own goals in life and her advocacy of homemaking and other traditional skills for young women and mothers. Her statements suggest that she really was firmly convinced that women could have both a career and a family.

In 1932 she told a Toledo, Ohio audience that a "modern mother may build a home and at the same time, have a career."[3] Four years later she reminded Girl Scout leaders at a regional conference in Duluth that "it is perfectly possible to have both a family and a career."[4] The fact that she was still advocating the importance of citizenship training and homemaking skills as late as 1939 suggests that she was aware of the fact that most young women of that day still thought of themselves as potential mothers and homemakers. In view of the current discussion of life on the "mommy track" and the impact of the women's movement on family life, her views certainly merit further investigation and discussion.

Her interest in outdoor activities for girls and young women spilled over from Girl Scouting into the establishment of the National Amateur Athletic Federation at the end of 1922. The 1920s and 1930s were a very important period in the history of men's and women's amateur sports.

Health care professionals in the early 1920s were very concerned about an apparent decline in the health and physical fitness of the average American. World War I and the international influenza epidemic of 1918-1919 had focused attention on public health problems and provided some sobering statistics. Large numbers of American men had been rejected for military service because of physical defects; and it was also discovered that rural health levels had slipped below those in the cities.

These disturbing disclosures, coupled with the realization that Americans were being lured by the appeal of spectator sports into ever increasingly sedentary lifestyles, prompted federal officials to seek solutions. A series of meetings and conferences led to the formation, on December 29, 1922, of the National Amateur Athletic Federation. In view of her well-known interest in outdoor recreation and activities for girls, Mrs. Hoover was chosen to be one of the NAAF's vice presidents—the only woman so honored. Aware of the many unique problems associated with women's athletics, the delegates agreed that NAAF should have separate divisions for men and women.

The issues confronting the Women's Division were numerous, involving many practical concerns along with profound differences of opinion on several philosophic issues. Practical concerns included the need for rules appropriate for girls' sports and the scarcity of space, facilities, qualified female coaches, equipment, and understanding and support on the part of community leaders.

An important debate ensued over such questions as the kinds and amounts of activity that were thought to be medically and philosophically advisable, the intensity of training and competition that ought to be allowed, and a definition of what constituted "serviceable, modest attire." Concern over these issues had already crystallized into a clash over the conduct of the international Olympic Games. Throughout its existence, the Women's Division of NAAF consistently opposed the participation of women and girls in the Olympics, feeling that both the manner in which the events were conducted and the emphasis on competition by highly trained, elite athletes was inappropriate.

The Women's Division merged with another organization in 1940 and survives today as the National Association for Girls and

Women in Sport. The debate over participation for all girls versus competition has not been resolved and there is still a lively discussion of the level of activity deemed medically advisable. Recent discussions of the safety of estrogen supplements have only carried the debate to a new level. Viewed in this larger context, the old questions that perplexed Lou Hoover and the other founders of the NAAF remain just as relevant today as they were seventy years ago.

During the postwar period (1918-1923) Herbert Hoover's wartime reputation as a worker of humanitarian miracles was further enhanced when he organized new relief organizations to save millions from famine, disease, and pestilence in Europe and Russia. Then came service as secretary of commerce. In 1927, he was called upon to deal with another disaster in the form of the greatest flood ever recorded in the Mississippi Valley. All of these led, inexorably, to the election of 1928, the White House, and four more years of service for Lou—this time as first lady.

As William Seale points out in his chapter, Lou Henry Hoover's tenure as first lady was unique. Unlike many of her predecessors, she had a sense of purpose and a devotion to service long before she became the nation's official mistress of ceremonies. Although she might have distained her ceremonial functions as trivial, she did not, choosing instead to raise them to a new level of hospitality, sensitivity, elegance, and grace. Nowhere was this more evident that in the area of culture and the arts.

Elise Kirk's examination of Lou's life-long interest in art and culture begins with her initial, surprisingly successful efforts as a teenage artist and author. (Rosemary Carroll has come to a similar conclusion in regard to Lou's early literary efforts.) Kirk provides us with numerous examples of Mrs. Hoover's cultural leadership ranging from her encouragement of American artists during the Depression to the rich musical fare offered at White House concerts and musicales during the Hoover administration.

Mrs. Hoover's success as official hostess came as no surprise to Washington's society reporters, who had known her for many years, or to her many friends who frequently wrote to express admiration for the gracious manner in which she made her guests comfortable. One act of hospitality, however, generated a firestorm of controversy that caught her by surprise.

It was a Washington tradition for the first lady to give a series of teas for congressional wives. The incoming class of 1929 congressmen included Oscar DePriest, a black representative from Chicago. When Mrs. Hoover invited Mrs. DePriest to one of the teas there was an immediate storm of protest. Bigots in both the North and South viciously attacked the first lady for having "defiled" the White House.

Mrs. Hoover had not intended to make a statement by inviting Mrs. DePriest; it was simply the kind and decent thing to do. Judging from the correspondence in her files, most Americans agreed with Lou's actions and warmly applauded her. Soon afterward the president, in a rare act of public defiance, made a point of inviting the black presidents of Hampton and Tuskeegee Institutes to dine with him.

Another unexpected development occurred when the Hoovers, attempting to escape from the oppressive heat of Washington's summers, built a retreat in the nearby Blue Ridge Mountains. Soon after their camp on the Rapidan was ready for occupancy, they became aware that there was no school for children in the area. There were very few families in the nearby mountain hollows and they were too poor to pay taxes which might have provided a school. The Hoovers built and equipped a school—with an attached apartment for the teacher—and hired an experienced teacher who was familiar with the special needs of Applachian families.

When the Hoovers left the White House in March 1933 they did not retire from public service. Mrs. Hoover, who had remained busy during the White House years with women's athletics and the Girl Scouts, resumed her service as a Girl Scout board member and served a second term as president from 1935-1937. At an age when many began to think about tapering off she became active in

11

several new organizations as one of the founders of the Friends of Music at Stanford University and as a regional officer of the Salvation Army.

Other organizations that claimed a part of her time included the American Red Cross, the Community Chest, Mills College, the San Francisco Opera Association, several Stanford University groups, Whittier College, Women's City Clubs, the Women's Overseas Service League, the Young Women's Christian Association, and a host of San Francisco and Palo Alto service and cultural organizations. Files reflecting her membership and involvement in these and dozens of other groups may be found in the Professional and Organizational Activities series of her papers.

Clearly she had lived a full and even adventurous life filled with many accomplishments and satisfaction. In eulogy following her death in 1944, her good friend Ray Lyman Wilbur sought to summarize her busy and productive life, offering the opinion that "there is no finer example of how to live than was given us by Lou Henry Hoover."

Chapter 1 ❧ Lou Henry Hoover: The Emergence of a Leader, 1874–1916

Rosemary F. Carroll

The ambition to do, to accomplish, irrespective of its measure in money or fame, is what should be inculcated. The desire to make the things that are, better, in a little way with what is at hand, — in a big way if the opportunity comes.[1]

Lou Henry Hoover wrote these lines during the early morning hours of November 25, 1914, just before sailing for England. She was about to cross the Atlantic in time of war; German U-boats infested the waters surrounding the British Isles, and Lou was aware that she would be in a dangerous situation from which she might not emerge safely. She therefore wanted to be certain that her sons, Herbert and Allan, knew the importance of a life of service. These lines also reflect the legacy of leadership through service that was evident in Lou Henry Hoover's life from her earliest years.

Qualities of leadership are often evident at an early age and so it was with Lou Henry Hoover. This chapter begins in 1874, the year of her birth, and culminates in 1916, the year she concluded her work as president of the Society of American Women in London.

Lou Henry Hoover was an unpretentious yet exceptional individual from childhood—intelligent, educated, and articulate. Reared by parents who prized education, the natural environment, and philanthropy as well as the values of industry, frugality, kindness, and compassion, Lou Henry Hoover was self-confident, adventuresome, practical, and independent—one who could do many things well and often simultaneously. She was a person who set her own agenda, an individual whose character and personality in adult life reflected leadership traits already evident in her childhood and adolescence.

Born on March 29, 1874, in Waterloo, Iowa, Lou was the elder of two daughters of Charles Delano Henry and Florence Weed Henry. Charles Henry was cashier for the First National Bank of Waterloo at the time of her birth. He followed a career in banking that eventually took him and his family to California, first to Whittier and then to Monterey. Florence Henry was a teacher by training, but due to her health and the family's growing affluence, she did not continue teaching.

Both parents gave a great deal of attention to Lou and her younger sister, Jean. When Lou was a student at Stanford her mother and father wrote to her almost daily and expected her to do the same. Lou and her parents often chided one another when the day's mail brought nothing. Her mother's letters centered on clothes, proper etiquette, sister Jean's musical talents and performances, and matters of health. Her father's letters usually concerned banking and personal finance. As a result, Lou developed an interest in financial matters as evidenced by the detailed account she kept while at Stanford of her expenses for everything from streetcar fare and shoe repairs to the purchase of cookies. The same careful attention that she applied to her academic work she carried over to her daily, weekly, and monthly expense recordings.

From reading the Henry family correspondence, one gains the impression that Charles Henry was a hard-working, intelligent man willing to take on new ventures, such as the opening of banks in Whittier and Monterey, California. Lou learned a great deal

A family portrait of Lou and her sons Allan (left) and Herbert taken in 1908, at the height of the "London years," by a London photographer.

about banking and the outdoors from her father. "I spent a great
deal of time with my father . . . as everything connected with the
banking business, and especially everything that he was doing, was
of great interest to me."[2] In Whittier Lou and her father often went
"tramping" and overnight camping.

> My father loved the mountains, and every moment that he could
> steal away from his indoor occupation, we went exploring and
> camping in what would be new country to us.[3]

Although her father had taken her hunting and fishing in her
younger years in Iowa, during her adolescence she spent much
more time with him in the California mountains. Through these
excursions Lou developed a great affinity for the outdoors and
nature, an interest that would prompt her work with the Girl
Scouts in her adult life.

An essay Lou wrote at the age of fifteen bears eloquent
testimony not only to her love of the outdoors but also to her
intelligence and powers of expression and observation. The essay,
entitled "How I Spent Vacation," also provides glimpses of
the sense of humor and zest for living that later became her
hallmark.

> For some time I had been planning a short trip to the mountains,
> and early on the morning of the second Tuesday in vacation our
> party started.
>
> Twelve of us, with enough provisions to last a fortnight, cold-
> hearted spectators said, were packed very conveniently in a large
> wagon, a supply of food was secured, our driver flourished his
> whip, the four horses started and we bid farewell to Whittier, our
> homes, and civilized life.
>
> To say that we had a jolly time would be expressing it very mildly
> indeed. The drive to the mountains was delightful. The fun we had
> while there, and the many wonderful things we saw indescribable.
>
> Our first days climb, our camp at the Half-way House, the
> glorious campfire, the delicious supper, beautiful moonlight and
> refreshing night's rest —the climb to the top, beautiful scenery

along the trail, grand view from the summit, our many excursions from Camp Utopia, the delightful evening spent around the campfire, enlivened by song and story, our serenade party, visits to the astronomical observatory, the descent, horse ride by moonlight and an hour spent at a Spanish fandango are among the many items which cannot be described in a "short concise description of how we spent vacation." Suffice to say that we arrived home safely, *rather* tanned but all perfectly delighted with our few days of mountaineering.[4]

Lou was in the first graduating class at the Bailey Street School in Whittier in 1890. That fall she enrolled at Los Angeles Normal School with the obvious intention of becoming a teacher, a field thought suitable for women in Victorian America. While at the Los Angeles Normal School she was a member and secretary of the Dickens Club, an extracurricular scientific group that focused on botany, zoology, microscopy, and taxidermy. Lou's notebook stated that the purpose of the club was to "make regular additions to the collections in Normal Museum."[5] The notebook also recorded that each member would keep drawings, that meetings would follow parliamentary procedure, that there would be field trips, and that the club would have an aquarium and a collection of "unique live pets."[6]

One observes here Lou's early interest in things scientific and her desire to increase her knowledge beyond the standard classroom curriculum, a trait that resurfaced in her Stanford days when she wrote to R.A.F. Penrose, Jr., of the Common Wealth Mining and Milling Company of Philadelphia requesting a copy of his article, "The Superficial Alteration of Ore Deposits." Lou obviously was interested in more than the basic requirements of a course. She was not going to content herself simply with the geological specimens found at Stanford or on field trips.

Lou was a serious student both in and out of the classroom but she also possessed a keen sense of humor. Her October 29, 1891 diary entry also reveals an interest in fair play.

All our trust in faithless mankind has fled! Miss Dunn has no one to defend her now, and serious threats are heard of tossing her in the canvas tomorrow. She "sprang" an examination in history upon us without the slightest warning! And not daring to stay and receive the brunt of our wrath she went to deliver a lecture away off somewhere, and left Miss Merritt to receive all our frowns and sighs. After school a general indignation meeting was held in Miss Monk's room, which was a little consoling.[7]

By 1891 Whittier's banking business, like the rest of the town's economy, was suffering from a depression. However, the reputation of Charles Henry as a banker of acumen resulted in his being asked to come to Monterey to open that city's first bank. Hence the Henrys moved to Monterey and Lou entered San Jose Normal School in the fall of 1892. After her graduation on June 23, 1893, she was still uncertain about whether she wished to teach. Instead she took a position "as an assistant cashier in the Monterey Bank"[8] until the spring of 1894 when the Monterey Board of Education asked her to be a substitute teacher for the remainder of the school year. Lou agreed to do so; however, a latent interest had been awakened in the spring of 1894 when she heard Professor John Casper Branner of Stanford University deliver a guest lecture on geology. Lou was fascinated with the prospect of studying geology with Branner; thus, in the fall of 1894 she enrolled at Stanford University.

When Lou entered Stanford, the university was a small, fledgling institution; its first class had been admitted in 1891. She pursued a liberal arts education with a major in geology. Notebooks from her Stanford years are filled with class notes from English, geology, chemistry, and other courses. While at Stanford she took many courses in geology with Branner. It was in a geology laboratory class that she met Herbert Hoover, Branner's laboratory assistant. Branner served as a mentor to both Lou and Herbert and was a close personal friend of both until his death in 1922.

It was, perhaps, her independent spirit that caused her to give no heed to the fact that geology was not, in late nineteenth-century

America, considered a proper field for a woman. Her very presence created something of a crisis in her first geology course. The young men in the class reportedly held a meeting to determine if it would be appropriate for Lou, a female, to go on the required class field trips. The young men decided that they would allow her to go once to see if she could manage without being an encumbrance. After the first field trip the young men decided that Lou had managed very well and was no trouble at all. Thereafter she regularly took part in all the class field trips. One suspects that her fellow male students did not know how much time Lou had spent in the outdoors and in the mountains nor did they realize how serious a geology student she was. Her ability and persistence bore fruit on May 25, 1898, when she received a bachelor of arts degree in geology from Stanford University, making her one of the first women in the United States to receive a degree in geology.

Lou's interest in geology continued well beyond her Stanford years. She conducted research on the gold mines of the ancient Egyptians and on the geology of the Red Sea and later published an article on John Milne, a famous British seismologist, in the March 1912 *Bulletin of the Seismological Society*. On her various travels throughout the world after her marriage, she contacted local colleges and governments and asked them to send geological specimens of their area to the Geology Department at Stanford. The following from the secretary of mines of the Government of Tasmania was typical: "I forward herewith a list of specimens of the ore and rocks of this State, which have been boxed and forwarded."[9] Branner was delighted with Lou's work as well as with some research she did for him at the British Museum in 1902. "Your efforts in our behalf are appreciated right up to the limit."[10] Thus, when Stanford opened its new geology building (the earlier one had been destroyed in the earthquake of 1906), the university had one of the most complete geology collections in the world— a fact that Branner duly attributed to the efforts of Lou Henry Hoover.

The practical side of Lou's nature is evident in her 1914 advice to her sons "to make the things that are, better, in a little way with what is at hand."[11] She was not a dreamer, an idler. Her approach was to attack a problem with the resources at hand. In her Stanford days, she wrote to her mother that in the matter of clothing, she wanted classic clothing, the type that was in good taste but simple and serviceable. Her diaries and letters from China are replete with remarks of how she was remaking an older outfit or hat. Lou's frugality was a family characteristic. Her letters from Stanford mentioned buying something in Palo Alto because it was less costly and admonishing her mother not to buy certain current magazines because Lou had discovered that those particular issues had nothing of interest. In her years in China she often wrote home asking the family to send magazines they had already read.

Lou had a remarkable ability to make people feel at ease in her company; furthermore, she could get diverse individuals to work together for a common goal. Nowhere was this more apparent than in her work as president of the Society of American Women in London. There is also clear evidence of her earlier popularity at Stanford in letters from classmates who wished to room with her or those who urged her to run for class president. She and Evelyn Wight Allan were largely responsible for the founding of the Kappa Kappa Gamma sorority chapter at Stanford in 1897. Evelyn had been elected national president of the sorority in 1891 and brought the idea of establishing a chapter to Stanford. Lou heard her speak; the chapter was established, and the two women began a lifelong friendship. Lou took a vital interest in the sorority's activities and maintained contact with many of her Kappa friends throughout her life.

Throughout her Stanford years, Lou's vitality, her academic competence, her love of the outdoors, and her popularity were joined with a special warmth and kindness toward others. The following incidents were typical. During her freshman year at Stanford, one of her classmates suffered from a severe case of neuralgia. Lou took the midnight to six AM shift to tend her ailing classmate. In her senior year, one of her classmates was a little short of funds to finish her education. Lou loaned her the money. This action was the predecessor of the education fund Lou would establish shortly after her marriage. She wrote to her father from China in 1899 that she wanted to set up a little educational fund to assist students who needed "just a little more to finish their education."[12] She continued:

> If you hear at any time of someone deserving who needs forty or fifty dollars "just to finish" a course or a year with, and there is not time to write me you can let them have it from this fund, and they can pay it back "at their convenience."[13]

It is clear that the money was to be repaid when the person was financially able to do so. The idea that one should work for what one received was important to Lou because in her judgment, the practice built good character and reflected a healthy mental attitude.

Upon graduation from Stanford Lou was soon exposed to the harsh realities of finding a job as a field geologist. Albert Whitaker, a Stanford friend, wrote to her in July 1898 about a conversation he had with Branner. Whitaker paraphrased Branner's remarks:

> Miss Henry is a good student of Geology. . . .Yes she did have an earnest purpose in taking Geology. Yes it was chiefly to do geodetic survey . . . work, original work that would be a new contribution to geological knowledge. She, undoubtedly, *would like* to pursue such work. But she cannot do it because she is a woman. The conventionalities of life do now and will continue to, for an indefinite period, to prevent it. . .
> Seriously, the field of original geological survey work is not open to women. But there is a field of geological labor where genuine contributions to the science might be made in which women have just as great an opportunity as men. (I cannot recall just what Dr. Branner named this branch of geology. But as I remember it, it was

the microscopic side of geology, and included the making of slides, etc.—microscopic investigation. I believe a kind of chemistry of geology. . . .)

Miss Henry is not fully prepared for this work. But if she wishes to accomplish the purpose of making original contribution to geology—"My advice to her," said Dr. Branner, "would be to take another year in college in preparation."[14]

Branner had already been making inquiries with the California Bureau of Mines, apparently hoping to secure a position for Lou or failing that, that she would return to Stanford to earn a master's degree and therefore be a stronger candidate for such a position.

However, a singularly important event intervened. Although her papers provide little information on the subject,[15] Lou and Herbert Hoover had "carried on a correspondence"[16] after his graduation in 1895. Herbert, whom Lou always called Bert, was employed in Australia as a mining engineer for the British firm of Bewick-Moreing. In 1898 C. Algernon Moreing, the senior partner in the firm, had agreed to send a mining engineer as consultant to Emperor Kwang Hsu of China, who was engaged in efforts to modernize his country. Moreing believed that Hoover was the man for the task. The Chinese agreed; Hoover accepted the appointment and cabled a brief proposal of marriage. Lou accepted Bert's proposal and they were married on February 10, 1899, in her family's home in Monterey with her parents and sister and his brother and sister in attendance. The following day Lou and Bert boarded the *Coptic* at San Francisco for their trip to China, specifically to the city of Tientsin, for Bert to take up his assignment.

Lou and Bert arrived in Tientsin in March 1899. The first year was a peaceful one in which Lou began the study of the Chinese language, visited Chinese cities and historic sites, went with Bert on mining expeditions, and began developing her interest in Chinese porcelains, the famous "blues and whites." At her father's request, she kept a diary of her observations on Chinese life and culture.

In the early months of 1900 a group of Chinese nationalists, known as the Boxers, launched a campaign to rid China of foreign influences. They murdered missionaries and Chinese Christians in a number of cities. The rebellion reached Tientsin in June 1900. The Hoovers were in the midst of a very dangerous situation because the foreign enclave would likely be a Boxer target. Bert suggested to Lou that she leave; she would have none of it. Rather, she stayed and assisted not only the foreigners but also the non-Boxer Chinese who had taken refuge in the foreign settlement.

The siege of Tientsin was a grim experience that tested Lou's character and courage. The danger was real and the Hoovers were aware of it. Later she wrote to Evelyn Wight Allan, "We simply had to stand by our guns until the end with one last bullet kept back for each one of ourselves."[17] Unlike others who huddled together in basements during the bombardment, however, Lou went about daily seeking food and standing guard at the barricades. On one occasion the tires of her bicycle were riddled by snipers' bullets[18] and on another she calmly continued playing solitaire in her living room while an artillery shell demolished part of a nearby staircase.[19] Another eyewitness later remarked that she seemed to "enjoy" the battle and did not worry about the danger all around.[20] Perhaps the best expression of her attitude can be found in her admonition to Evelyn Wight Allan: "You missed one of the opportunities of your life by not coming to China in the summer of 1900 . . . you should have been here,—at the most interesting siege of the age."[21]

Lou's actions in the face of the Boxer peril reflected not only personal courage but also the initiative to take positive action as seen in her various efforts to be of service during the crisis. By mid-July, after terrible destruction not only to the foreign settlement but also to Chinese shops and homes, the siege was lifted by an international force of foreign troops.[22] The Hoovers began writing a book detailing their experiences, but it was never finished. Fortunately, the project had reached a very advanced stage before it was abandoned and the drafts have survived in her papers.

Lou and Bert divided the fall of 1900 between London and Monterey. However, by December 1900, they were back in the Orient—Bert in China and Lou and her sister, Jean, in Japan. The two women went to Tientsin in April 1901 and remained there until the following fall. Lou, Bert, and Jean then returned to London because Bert had been made a partner in the firm of Bewick-Moreing.

The London years, 1902-1916, were extraordinarily rich and full ones in Lou's life. During that period she circled the world five times; established homes in London and California; gave birth to sons Herbert, born August 4, 1903, and Allan, born July 17, 1907; entertained a host of friends; published articles and worked on reminiscences of China; translated, with Bert, Georgius Agricola's *De Re Metallica*; actively engaged in philanthropy; and was a vibrant force in the Society of American Women in London. All the while she maintained a close family relationship with her husband and children, her parents, her sister, Jean, and other relatives and friends. Her diaries, correspondence, and related materials reveal a great deal about her character, personality, and emerging qualities of leadership.

Lou's most sustained academic project during the London years was the translation of Agricola's *De Re Metallica*, an important sixteenth-century textbook on mining and metallurgy that had long baffled scholars who had attempted to translate it. Preserving the technology was one of their aims. The problem largely lay in the fact that the work was written in Latin and no Latin words existed for many of the processes Agricola was attempting to explain. Rather than use the vernacular German of his day, Agricola invented new Latin terms, which made the work very difficult to translate. The translation clearly required the efforts of those with knowledge of the Latin language and also of the science of mining and geology. The Hoovers were the ideal candidates to perform this task; Lou was an excellent Latinist; Bert was a mining engineer, and they were both well acquainted with geology and metallurgy.

Lou and Bert had been aware of this document since their Stanford days when Dr. Branner introduced them to it. They were eager to undertake the translation, perhaps little realizing how formidable and lengthy a project it would be. The translation would ultimately consume much of their free time from 1907 to 1912. The result of Lou and Bert's five-year effort was the production, based on the first Latin edition of 1556, of a 598-page translation of *De Re Metallica* with several appendices and copious footnotes. The extensive footnotes were a Hoover addition since none appeared in the original text.

Translating *De Re Metallica* into English presented formidable problems because many of the mining processes described had never been practiced in the English-speaking world; other processes were obsolete. In addition, there was the need to avoid the use of modern technical terms that would give a false depiction of the state of the science in the sixteenth century. Despite these obstacles, Lou and Bert forged ahead because they recognized the importance of the work; it was the bible of mining. More than a translation, Lou and Bert's work "placed Agricola in the scientific and cultural background of his time."[23]

Three thousand copies of the Hoovers' translation were published in 1912 with a price of only one-fifth of its printing cost so that it could be "within the reach of all interested parties."[24] Here again one finds evidence of the Hoovers' generosity as well as in the fact that they gave several copies as gifts to friends, libraries, museums, and universities all over the globe. Appropriately enough, the Hoovers dedicated their work to Dr. Branner: "The inspiration of whose teaching is no less great than his contribution to science."[25] The Mining and Metallurgical Society of America in 1914 presented Lou and Bert with the society's first Gold Medal for their outstanding scholarly achievement in making Agricola's *De Re Metallica* accessible to the modern world.

Lou had been no stranger to philanthropic work. Her early inclination in this direction led her to lend money to one of her Stanford classmates. Shortly after her graduation from Stanford,

Lou and her mother were instrumental in founding the Monterey-Pacific Grove Chapter of the American Red Cross during the Spanish-American War of 1898.

During the London years she was a member of The Friends of the Poor, an organization designed "by personal service to assist deserving families in times of distress" and "to place poor boys and girls in satisfactory situations upon leaving school."[26] Several interesting examples of her philanthropy may be found in her papers. On October 17, 1912, the secretary, A. N. Collin, sent Lou a letter stating:

> You were kind enough to say you would visit a family for us and we are enclosing particulars of the Coppingers living at 6, Rickett Street, Fulham.... After you have been and visited perhaps you will come up and see us and talk over the best way of helping them.[27]

The Coppinger family consisted of a husband and wife, both age 32, and their children ranging in age from 1 month to 4 years. The husband was an unemployed chauffeur. Lou visited the family and recommended him to the General Omnibus Company for employment, but at the time, there was no vacancy. Lou, about to make a trip to the United States, gave £10 per week for the family until her return.

Lou also belonged to the Lyceum Club, an international organization, when she and Bert lived in London. The club was originally organized to promote a wide-ranging array of lectures, concerts, and debates. By 1915 it had also formed the Lyceum League for Help in Time of War to render assistance to the wounded and to other groups working to relieve distress that resulted from the First World War. Lou's membership in the Society of American Women in London, however, was to be the vehicle for her most systematic philanthropic work during the London years.

The Society of American Women in London was founded in 1899 and became a member of the General Federation of Women's

Clubs in 1900. The idea of a club for American women resident in London grew out of a meeting in November 1898 at the home of Mrs. Hugh Reid Griffin who had recently been appointed regent of the Daughters of the American Revolution. Mrs. Daniel Manning, president general of the Daughters of the American Revolution, thought a DAR chapter could be established in London. Neither Mrs. Griffin nor the American ambassador thought it the proper time to establish a DAR chapter; however, the idea of bringing together American women in London in an organized fashion grew out of this meeting. The Society of American Women in London was formed and kept that name until 1916 when it became the American Women's Club. The Constitution of the society stated:

> The object of the Society is to promote social intercourse between American women, and to bring together women who are engaged in literary, artistic, scientific and philanthropic pursuits.[28]

In 1908 Lou was nominated for membership. Mrs. Webster Glynes, the second president of the Society, wrote to Lou: "I am very pleased you are joining our Society."[29] One can easily see why Lou wanted membership in the Society of American Women in London. The object or purpose of the organization fit nicely with her own educational and philanthropic values. The fact that the society had provided a hospital ship to the Allied forces during the Boxer Rebellion doubtless increased Lou's interest in the society. Once a member, she became very active and influential in the society's work.

Shortly after she joined the society, Lou became a member of its Education and Philanthropic Committee, first as a committee member and later as its chair. This committee was important for a variety of reasons, one of which was that it administered a scholarship fund for needy students. The committee also supplied Easter Sunday dinner for the poor of East London; gave financial help to those in distress; helped support elderly women; helped subsidize the Browning Settlement, a home for the indigent; and held an annual tea to secure funds and toys for needy children at the Browning Settlement and the Notting Hill Day Nursery. The annual report of the committee in 1913 noted that Lou had made a financial donation to support the work of the committee.

Throughout the year the society had luncheons and Salon Lectures for which Lou was one of the organizers. In 1913 the Salon Lectures were on China, Swinburne, and the causes of the French Revolution, the latter lecture given by Hilaire Belloc. Other lectures concerned Bergson's philosophy, the Balkans, education in India and Ceylon, and the issue of women's suffrage in the United States. Lou obviously relished the kind of intellectual stimulation these lectures provided and enjoyed her work on the Education and Philanthropic Committee.

The Society of American Women in London also sponsored weekly sightseeing trips in London to visit such sights as the British Museum, Soane Museum, Dr. Barnardo's Home for Boys, and the Norman Church of St. Bartholomew the Great, the oldest church in London. Going on these trips was of great value to Lou in that she became familiar with key sights in the city to show her many visitors to London. The visit to the British Museum included a lecture on porcelain, china, and pottery, all of which were of great interest to Lou who had already begun the systematic collection of Chinese "blues and whites" from the Ming and K'ang Hsi dynasties.

Lou was quick to welcome society members into her home. On June 29, 1913, the society's corresponding secretary, Lucy Allen Selwyn, wrote to Lou:

> The entire success of the entertainment was due to your efforts and we heartily thank you for your always ready assistance and cooperation in plans to forward on the work of the Society.[30]

Lou was clearly a valued and respected member of the society for her spirit of helpfulness and gracious hospitality. In 1910 Mrs. William Righter Comings, the president, invited her to run for the office of first vice president:

> I hope you will not think me very audacious in what I am going to ask of you. I have the hearty concurrence of all the Committee in asking if you will accept nomination for 1st Vice President of the Society of American Women. . . . If you feel at all doubtful in accepting may I not come to talk to you Thursday next week.[31]

Mrs. Comings was clearly anxious to have Lou run, but she need not have worried. Lou accepted and won the election. The first vice presidency was an important post because with it came membership on the Executive Committee, which set the society's agenda; in addition, the first vice president was first in the line of succession to the presidency.

Lou was re-elected first vice president in 1912. When that term concluded in 1914, Mrs. Comings wrote to Lou asking her to run again for first vice president. Lou declined saying that the Constitution of the society prevented a third term. Mrs. Comings, however, in a liberal reading of the Constitution, again wrote to Lou that the prohibition of a third term pertained only to the office of the president: "As to the 'third term' precedent I think that applies very forcibly to the President. I personally do not think it applies to the other officers."[32] Mrs. Comings urged Lou to run. "I want to ask you if you will not reconsider your decision not to stand. It is distinctly the wish of the Club."[33] At the time Lou was in the United States with Bert and the children visiting her parents. Finally she agreed to accept the nomination for a third term; this was an important decision as events, not anticipated in January 1914, would demonstrate.

Lou won reelection to the first vice presidency handily in 1914 but her tenure in that office would be brief. Still in California, Lou received a cable on May 24, 1914: "Mrs. Griffiths resigning Presidency American Society because death husband you thus become President."[34] With the resignation of Mrs. Griffiths, Lou became president at the outbreak of the First World War, right at the time when she could marshal the resources of the society in support of the Allied cause.

In a report to American Ambassador Walter Hines Page, Bert told him that on August 3, 1914, the consul general had informed him of the "acute destitution that had arisen among travelling Americans, as a result of the declaration of war, and the consequent declaration of a series of five Bank Holidays."[35] Bert plunged into the crisis by forming the American Committee to aid stranded Americans. Lou immediately mobilized her friends in the Society of American Women in London and formed the Women's Division of the American Committee. With Bert as chair of the American Committee and Lou as chair of the Women's Division, relief was quickly organized for more than 120,000 Americans who were attempting to return to the United States.

The Society of American Women in London made the Women's Division of the American Committee a standing subcommittee in 1914. In addition to the society's usual philanthropies, it established a knitting factory in Islington where "its influence . . . is already much marked, and we much hope that it may develop into a permanent settlement."[36] The Society also offered courses in first aid, home nursing, and cooking.

During Lou's term as president of the Society of American Women in London from 1914 to 1916 her talents as a leader and organizer soon became apparent to her fellow members. She organized relief committees of various sorts, left detailed written instructions with other officers of the society when she was going to be out of London, and traveled to Belgium and Germany with Bert on behalf of the Commission for Relief in Belgium. While in the United States in October and November 1914, she not only put young Herbert and Allan in school but also raised funds and addressed rallies in support of the Commission for Relief in Belgium, which Bert now chaired.

Lou was back in England in early December 1914. By January 1915 she was fast at work on the variety of tasks facing her as president of the Society of American Women in London. There was much to do, particularly in the area of philanthropy. She quickly recruited the Duchess of Marlborough,[37] who was her friend, to chair the society's philanthropic committee. Lou wrote:

> Of course, it goes without saying that if you accepted the Chairmanship of this, its one great Committee, I should feel my power greatly strengthened in making this organization one worthy of the name "American," and I should personally be very grateful.[38]

The Duchess accepted the nomination and won the election. It is very evident in this letter that Lou intended her presidency to be one of vigor, one that would make the Society of American Women in London a very strong organization with a priority on philanthropy. As she wrote to Mrs. Griffiths:

> We have also decided for the present six months (and it will no doubt be continued) to turn all fees and dues of income of members into a philanthropic work. It was really the only way I could consent to take on the work as President."[39]

With her friend the Duchess of Marlborough as chair of the Philanthropic Committee, Lou raised funds for the various philanthropies, supervised activities at the knitting factory at Islington, and wrote numerous letters to the other officers regarding their work.

She was especially interested in the establishment of a maternity hospital in Belgium. The constitution of the society did not permit using society funds for activities in countries outside the British Isles. Lou wrote to the Duchess and other Executive Committee members that she had received a donation of £250 "to be used towards the establishment and upkeep of a much needed maternity center or temporary hospital in Flanders."[40] Lou never said from whence the donation came; one suspects it came from her own resources. In any case, the Executive Committee agreed the funds could be used for a special purpose such as this one; hence, the hospital was established.

In reviewing the society's activities, Lou's presidential report for 1915 noted:

> The activities of the Society of American Women in London covered a wider field during the past year, 1915, than even before. . . . Naturally, the ordinary functions of the club were in little demand while the extraordinary ones flourished. The Rooms at Whitehall Court saw little formal entertaining, but much of the Committees and Red Cross classes, and Reports from the Workers at the various "Fronts."[41]

The report then referred to the society's membership, which had increased by twenty-five new members since 1914 making a total of one hundred ninety-one members. On finances Lou wrote in great detail, reminiscent of how precisely she kept track of her expenditures when a student at Stanford. She noted how the entrance fees, dues, and special donations, as well as nearly $5,000 of U. S. government funds, all went into the various philanthropic enterprises of the society. For example, the knitting factory, the maternity hospital, the education committee, the philanthropic committee, and the American Women's War Relief Fund, as well as the Women's Division of the American Committee, were all beneficiaries, as were other smaller charities, of the monies collected.

In her report for 1915 Lou reviewed the work of the committees, such as the Education Committee that assisted parents in the selection of schools, placed poor children in appropriate facilities, and provided guidance and financial support for some American children caught in England because of the war. Lou reminded members that "good, outgrown, but not outworn, school clothing and supplies . . . are always most acceptable to this Committee."[42]

Lou pointed out that the knitting factory "has given work to nearly one hundred women on the very verge of starvation—

beyond the boundary of simple hunger"[43] and that the factory has sold nearly seven hundred pounds worth of what it produced and "has given away many hundreds of articles to hospitals, institutions, the men at the Front and in the Fleet."[44] Lou also indicated that many of the women working at the factory were elderly and

> that if they left the Factory today there would be no hope for them but the workhouse. While the war lasts and there is the present demand for hand-knitted and machine-knitted goods, this work will doubtless continue to be self-supporting—if friends are generous with running expenses, food, heat, lighting ... as in the past.[45]

One notes both here and in her remarks about the education committee that Lou made a plea for clothing and funds. She also mentioned the American Benevolent Committee, a group formed in late 1915 to solicit and allocate funds to the various committees dealing with distressed Americans in England. She told members she hoped they "subscribed liberally"[46] to the American Benevolent Committee and, if they had not, "It is still not too late!"[47] By the end of her term the society had become a strong and vibrant force.

From childhood Lou had been encouraged by her parents to take on new challenges and to use her talents in the service of others. She had been nurtured in a value system that emphasized consideration for those less fortunate than herself, planning for the future, exercising leadership and making the most of one's opportunities; but most of all, being of service to others.

In her youth she met a partner, Herbert Hoover, who embraced the same philosophy of generous and unselfish service. He admired her kindness and compassion, respected her abilities, and encouraged her activities in behalf of others. In each phase of her life from 1874 until 1916 she made distinct contributions by the strength of her character, by the generosity of her nature, by the unstinting use of her talents, and by the gentle and gracious quality of her personality.

Just a few weeks after her graduation from Stanford University, Lou Henry Hoover had written to her friend Evelyn Wight (Allan) concerning the remarks made by David Starr Jordan, president of Stanford, at the Commencement luncheon.

> In speaking of his personal "beacon moments" of the year, he said the strongest were when he found Stanford students at work in remote corners of the world, so that our influence thro' them was felt in all quarters of the globe from Alaska to South America—in Africa, Australia, China, and Europe.[48]

Although Lou most probably, at the time, did not realize it, these words would find fulfillment in the many public services she later performed. In 1914 she stood on the brink of a career of public service; by 1916 she had become proficient in the qualities of quiet, behind-the-scenes leadership that would become her hallmark as a national Girl Scout leader and later as first lady.

Chapter 2 ❧ "Don't Forget Joy!" Lou Henry Hoover and the Girl Scouts

Rebecca Christian

To look at pictures taken late in life of First Lady Lou Henry Hoover unsmiling in her carefully ironed Girl Scout uniform and sturdy brogans, you might imagine that scouting, to her, was rules and badges and lining grimly up to march.

Not so, as a turn through her personal papers at the Herbert Hoover Presidential Library in West Branch and at the archives of the Girl Scouts USA in New York City reveals. In fact, her constant message to leaders was "Don't forget joy!"

In reminiscences of Lou Hoover in oral histories taken from her contemporaries at scout headquarters in New York, a portrait of a lively, friendly, democratic leader emerges. The anecdotes show her stretching out on a forest floor for a nap, knitting restlessly during meetings, taking leaders on a "fern walk," and sitting on the floor Indian-style, telling stories of her adventurous California girlhood to a group of spellbound Brownies. Many of the stories about her gently persuasive style illustrate her philosophy of leadership: "Lead from behind."

The Girl Scout organization, of which Mrs. Hoover was an

ardent supporter and leader from the time she was handpicked by
the movement's founder, Juliette Gordon Low, in 1917 until her
death in 1944, was a natural for the lithe, athletic geologist and
conservationist.

Born Lou Henry in Waterloo, Iowa, on March 29, 1874, she
was the older of two girls and a tomboy. Unlike a typical upper
middle-class little girl in the Victorian era, she was taught by her
adored father, Charles Henry, to enjoy horseback riding, camping,
hunting, woodcraft, and geology as if she was the son he never had.

She came naturally by the independence she was to exhibit both
in the Girl Scout movement and throughout her remarkable life.
Her grandmother homesteaded in Dakota Territory, and her
mother Florence Henry, had been a schoolteacher and had lived an
active life as a farm girl.

As Lou Hoover told the annual conference of the Covered
Wagon Region of Girl Scouts in Davenport, Iowa, on April 28,
1937:

> "And of course it is a great joy for me to be coming to a Girl Scout
> gathering in Iowa, for I did my very first Scouting in my world right
> here in Iowa! My first camping was done over in Blackhawk
> County. My first cooking and eating out of doors was there—I can't
> even remember when. My first sleeping out all night, under the
> stars, was there—where we had to have a tent nearby to run to in
> case of thunderstorms, —real thunderstorms they were too. And I
> learned to paddle a canoe and fish on the Cedar River, and owned
> my first little rowboat there—aged about ten.[1]

Of course, the range of Mrs. Hoover's interests and accomplishments went way beyond the Girl Scouts. She was the first woman
to earn a geology degree from Stanford University (1898); she
was the first author of a comprehensive history of White
House furnishings (1929); and she was the first president's wife to
invite a black woman to the traditional White House tea for
congressional wives, a gesture for which she was both reviled and
lauded.

Her sense of duty also led her to participate in a wide range of

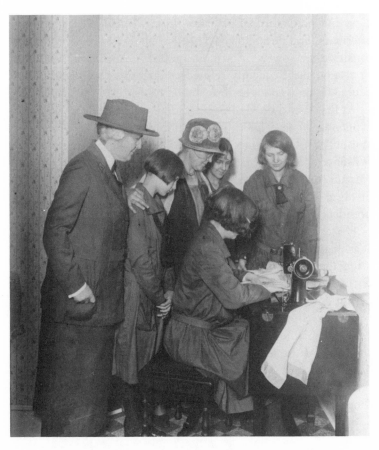

As President of the Girl Scouts (1922–1925) Lou took a very personal interest in her girls, encouraging them to freely explore their interests and to become responsible citizens and homemakers. Here she observed a 1925 sewing project.

civic and philanthropic activities during World War I and its aftermath, and during the Depression; but it was the Girl Scout organization, however, that most completely claimed her heart. As first lady, she frequently refused to give speeches—unless she could talk only about her beloved Girl Scouts.

As first lady, Lou Hoover was honorary president of the Girl Scouts as all first ladies since Edith Wilson (Mrs. Woodrow Wilson) have been. In fact, it was Lou Hoover who persuaded Mrs. Wilson to accept the post. While in the White House, Lou Hoover was not simply a figurehead for the Girl Scouts but an active and involved leader as she was both before and after her husband's presidency.

Her career with the Scouts began as acting commissioner in Washington, D.C., in 1917 and 1918, and she was also a troop leader there from 1922 to 1932. As leader, she allowed the girls to dig up her backyard for a garden, and as first lady, enlisted their help at government and White House functions.

She was also a council member (1923–1927, 1933–1944) in Palo Alto, California, which the Hoover family used as home base; chairman of the national board of directors (1925–1928); national president for two terms (1922–1925); and honorary vice president (1933–1944). In a memorial booklet written by the Girl Scouts after Lou Hoover's death, a former member of her Troop 8 reminisced:

> Troop 8 was made up of fifteen- to eighteen-year-old girls who were members of other troops but worked with Mrs. Hoover as a group to be called upon for participation in civic demonstrations, parades, international conferences, and so forth. We served at international Scout luncheons, demonstrated Scouting to the public and perhaps were the first Senior Service troop.
>
> Mrs. Hoover was the ideal leader for this group. We were fired with her enthusiasm and most of us acted as assistants in other troops or went as junior counselor to summer camps. I have never been able to leave Scouting—for she made us feel that we grew best as we served others.

She was genuinely interested in all of us. We could see her at any time, all during her Washington days. Every graduation day—high school, college, and postgraduate—brought each of us flowers, telegrams, or cards. Even our wedding and our babies were a source of interest to her.

She taught me enough about birds for me to pass my Bird Finder badge at the National Museum; encouraged me to know more and more trees by observing those in her garden and the streets near her home; and when I was working on my nature badges, took me all through her house, where we held our meetings, and made me tell the source, method of processing, and reason for using practically every metal or stone piece in her home—and she knew her geology.[2]

Mrs. Hoover's interest in scouting began in World War I when she worked side by side with the future president feeding the starving children of Europe. It was then that the young mother of two sons began to realize that she wanted to continue to work for the welfare of children after peace was declared and she returned to the United States.

In a long and reflective letter to Mrs. Paul Rittenhouse, then national director of the Girl Scouts, on July 1, 1936, the careful study the scholarly Mrs. Hoover made before committing herself to the organization is revealed:

I worked with the Girl Scouts *very* casually until the end of the War—because things to do for them just turned up under my hand. I was Acting Commissioner of Washington during 1917–1918. Following 1919, feeling that I might decide to continue some work with children, I myself made a very careful study of the programs of the more prominent organizations dealing with recreational and educational activities of high school aged young people—and of the upper grammar grades. I was not then so attached to the Girl Scouts that I would not readily have made a post-war affiliation instead with one of the other groups if I felt it had the possibility of better accomplishment.

And I found at that time there was just no comparison possible between the Girl Scouts and any other organization of its class—

either in program or volunteer personnel of staff. (And, as a comparison, this includes the Boy Scouts, too.)

For the next ten years I knew very intimately the development of the Girl Scouts and of the other "character building agencies," as they came to be called, for the same age young people.

The Girl Scouts were the pioneers in most of the fields. Checking back through their histories, you will find surprisingly often that the others were following with each new development—months, or years, after.[3]

Among the aspects of scouting that appealed to Mrs. Hoover were the commitment to outdoor and physical activities and community service and the wholesome use the organization made of the girls' leisure time. She was often to say how much she loved the Girl Scout's promises, laws, and mottos: to do her duty to God and her Country, to help other people at all times, to be prepared and to do a good turn daily. In a speech to the Daughters of the American Revolution in 1927, she appealed to them to consider becoming leaders and summed up her own feelings about scouting:

It seems to me that Girl Scouting is the best method of self-expression for girls; It makes them want to do the things they should do. I consider it one of the most worthwhile things on which I can spend that part of my day which is not imperatively demanded by my individual responsibilities to my family, my friends, my community and my nation.

One had certain overt or demanding duties to all of these; and beyond them one has further time and energy which we have grown to call "service" but which so often should be called "joy" instead; for being a Girl Scout leader, as we older ones are called, has as much joy in it, I can assure you, as being a Girl Scout.

So it might be said that the Girl Scouts' achievement is to have a good time while they are learning many of the ways of the older folk who work and play together—ways of being good homemakers, good citizens, good neighbors, and good comrades—which means a learning to keep a high courage and a stout and understanding heart and an alert mind in a sound, strong body.[4]

In the early days of Girl Scouting, Mrs. Hoover and her fellow leaders had their work cut out for them in educating the public about the fledgling movement; the organization was only five years old when she joined it in 1917. A brief history lesson puts those days in context. The Girl Scouts, now regarded as a traditional symbol of long-held American values, was a groundbreaking, even controversial organization then.

When Lou Hoover first became active in scouting, the notion of little girls tramping around in the woods sent shudders down genteel spines. Juliette Gordon Low's girls in Savannah had to pull a big canvas curtain around their athletic field to keep from scandalizing passersby with a glimpse of their bloomers.

The Girl Scouts were the Americanized version of the Girl Guides in England, which developed from the Boy Scouts that Lord Robert Baden-Powell founded in 1907. Baden-Powell was a major general who had become a hero because he was able to defend Mafeking during the Boer War in South Africa from 1899 to 1902, despite famine and sickness in his ranks.

During his years in the British army, he became convinced that young men from industrial cities like Liverpool needed more physical training and experience in outdoor life. In 1909, he and his sister responded to requests for a similar girls' organization by founding the Girl Guides.

Baden-Powell was definitely the man of the hour at the turn of the century; he was thronged by admirers wherever he went. In 1911, he met Juliette Gordon Low, a Georgia-born belle who was then the lonely widow of a wealthy British playboy. With Baden-Powell's blessing, Mrs. Low exported the Girl Guide movement to the United States. And without his blessing (Baden-Powell found the notion of female scouts unfeminine), she renamed it the Girl Scouts.

Lou Hoover, although she greatly respected Baden-Powell for formally codifying instinctive, centuries-old rules for young people to live by, stoutly defended Low's change of the organization's name. She thought the name symbolized the pioneering American spirit. In a speech before the Daughters of the American Revolution on April 22, 1927, she said, "They are Scouting out, as it were, into this civilization of ours, into the oncoming years, as did those Scouts of a century ago into our unknown continent. Hence the magic of the name."[5]

When Low started the movement in Savannah in 1912, the name change was not the only uphill climb she had to make. The Girl Scouts was the only women's organization in uniform besides nurses. Many of the leaders of the new movement were unmarried college graduates with a desire for social service, who—often for the first time—were working without the leadership of a male committee, minister, or priest.

An excerpt from the Girl Scout magazine, *The American Girl,* in April 1922, illustrates the attitudes of the era:

> One of the most amusing ideas is that deep seated one which is shared by all men: that a woman cannot drive a nail. . . . Of course she uses a hairpin if nobody gives her a screw driver, and of course she uses a hair brush or a slipper heel if she's not allowed to use a hammer. But give her a chance at the right way and see how long she'll choose the wrong one.[6]

World War I gave the Scouts an opportunity to show how capable they were. The war brought enormous attention to the organization. Girl Scouts held parades and flag ceremonies, sold Liberty Bonds, knitted sweaters and socks for soldiers, and set up kindergartens so mothers could work in war-related industries.

Seeing the scouts in action in London and Washington, D.C., during and just after the war, helped make Lou Hoover a believer in the organization. Although she appreciated the scouts' efforts during the war, she disliked the resultant military atmosphere that prevailed in the early days of scouting. She quietly discouraged drilling, marching, and signaling among her own girls, and it was partly her idea to change from a soldierly khaki uniform to a softer green. She wrote to a friend, Katherine Everts, on March 26, 1925,

"That military, hard-and-fast organization type is all very well for those who like it—and I don't happen to."[7]

When rivalries inevitably arose between the Boy Scout and Girl Scout organizations, Lou Hoover privately opined that the Girl Scouts were much more democratic and that its national head-quarters were more responsive to suggestions from the field. At the annual Girl Scout convention in Boston in 1934, she told leaders, "National is only a certain focal point of yourselves. We are always repeating, 'don't forget that you are National. . . . That you decide and control its actions.'"[8]

She also protested a move that was under way in the 1930s to lump all the national girls organizations under one umbrella. In a interview in the *Portland Tribune,* her exasperation with that idea is clear: "The fathers of these girls have hundreds of organizations. There are Lions and Elks and Rotarians and many, many others. Why should there not be as many for their daughters? And they do not overlap, we find."[9]

Perhaps Lou Hoover's most significant contribution to the scouts was the way she used her connections to strengthen the Girl Scout movement, whether recruiting leaders or undertaking the "despised [fund-raising] drives." Because the early scout leaders were shaping the organization as they went along, it was up to them to search in relevant fields like women's athletics, drama and medicine for energetic and capable women who might help to develop the organization's emerging program.

One of Lou Hoover's recruits was Lillian Gilbreth, the engineer and efficiency expert who was the model for the mother in the novel *Cheaper by the Dozen,* which was written by her children. On April 14, 1930, Lou Hoover suggested Dr. Gilbreth as a candidate for national director in a letter she wrote from the White House to Genevieve Brady:

> She has done a great deal of work remodeling old and setting up new engineering organizations and industrial plants, so that she has a very good idea of the co-ordination of departments and the work

43

of such a plant as ours when it is devoted to industrial products instead of to girls. . . .

And she is one who gets much accomplished. I have known her for many years. She has a dynamic personality, is a most interesting speaker, and carries an audience most convincingly.

She is very interested in the children's and young people's development and has studied modern tendencies very carefully. She is raising a family of eleven children herself most satisfactorily.

Incidentally, she is the most intelligently interested in Girl Scouting. When she was spending a weekend with me last autumn, we took a three-hour drive through the country and spent most of our time discussing educational and youthful problems—a great deal of it as pertaining to Girl and Boy Scouting. And our ideas are very similar in these lines.

She "wears" much better than her first impression. She is so frightfully busy and intent on things that she does not take the time or interest in superficialities—which sometimes are useful. I think everyone is surprised after she has been on her feet three minutes in speaking or after they have met her a short time in conversation, to discover how much more interesting she is than she promised to be.[10]

In 1927, Mrs. Hoover persuaded a publicity-shy Grace Coolidge, then first lady, to attend a Washington, D.C., Scout affair, thus thrilling many little girls in green. During the same era, it was largely through her influence that a generous grant for leader training came from the Laura Spelman Rockefeller Memorial.

The result was that between 1922 and 1927, training courses were installed in 155 colleges and institutions of higher learning in 42 states. About 10,000 young women took these courses. Lou Hoover herself spent the hot summer of 1922 visiting these leader-training camps. And when the grant money dried up, she persuaded old colleagues at Stanford University to offer a leader training course there.

Her beliefs about the importance of such training come through in a 1923 letter she wrote to a would-be scout leader in Paducah, Kentucky:

I always feel, in connection with Girl Scouting, in going into a new area, that it is so much better to have a number of the right type of leaders ready to devote a few hours a week to it, understandingly, before an appeal is made to the little girls to become Girl Scouts— or to their mothers and teachers to encourage the movement.... We so often find that the enthusiasm of the children is largely quenched by the inability to provide them with suitable and somewhat trained leaders to work with them.[11]

When she spoke to leaders, Lou Hoover's suggestions were many and practical, including "leading from behind," not enlisting mothers and teachers as leaders (too "bossy" and "school teacherish") and not raising money if it wasn't needed. She also urged leaders to talk to the girls about values, "for instance, the greater desirability of being right than of being outwardly, even glitteringly successful."[12]

The organization and its trappings of headquarters and archives and training manuals, she always contended, was not as important as the girls who composed it. "The girl's the thing!" she exclaimed. "First, foremost and always!"[13]

In addition to helping develop the Girl Scout movement and training leaders for it, Lou Hoover made myriad other contributions. Crises like the flu epidemic of 1918 and the Depression found her mobilizing her beloved scouts to help in the world beyond home and school. Within the organization, she helped pioneer the Lone Scout program so that girls in sparsely populated areas—like she lived in as she was growing up—could become scouts without joining a troop. And she helped develop Girl Scout Little Houses, many of which still exist. These were cabins, dugouts and other structures scouts could use to furnish, landscape, cook, meet, and camp in.

Because Lou Hoover rejected feminist activism that she viewed as extreme in earlier days, it's possible that with the Girl Scouts she set out to create a more conservative model of feminism that stressed competence as mother and homemaker as well as competence as athlete and nature lover. On the other hand, the outdoor programs of both the National Amateur Athletic Federation and the Girl Scouts, which she so enthusiastically promoted, sometimes represented a departure from activities for girls and women considered "proper" at the time. Under her tenure, the Girl Scout agenda that emerged emphasized self-discovery and new vocations for women which would seem to challenge more conventional views of the roles of women in her day.

Although she hated fund-raising, she helped convince trustees of the American Relief Administration to establish a $50,000 publications fund for Girl Scouts in 1925 and persuaded them to give another $500,000 to the organization over five years for an outdoor campaign and for leader training. A vintage photo shows her holding a box of Girl Scout cookies in one of the first national cookie campaigns.

It was camping, however, that the woman who had grown up a tomboy most loved. When she was elected president of the Girl Scouts in Savannah, Georgia, in 1922, she told them:

> To me the Outing part of Scouting has always been the most important. The happiest part of my own very happy childhood and girlhood was without doubt the hours or days, the sometimes entire months, which I spent in pseudo-pioneering, or scouting, in our wonderful western mountains with my father in our vacation times. So I cannot but want every girl to have the same widening, simplifying, joy-getting influences in her own life. . . .
>
> We don't want the girl of the small town to know Nature only from the seat of a Ford or a Dodge—or a Pierce Arrow, or a mossy log by a big lunch basket!
>
> Captains, when you go back to your troops, don't forget the "fun" part of scouting, and as far as possible, encourage the outdoor fun.[14]

One of Lou Hoover's favorite badges was the rock finder, which, as you might expect from the first woman to earn a geology degree from Stanford University, she helped to write. She was always surprised how many girls preferred homemaking badges to outdoor ones.

Because she believed that informal outdoor settings helped enhance meetings, she often invited colleagues to Camp Rapidan, the woodsy presidential retreat that she and Herbert Hoover built in the Blue Ridge Mountains. The love of the outdoors remained strong until the end of her life, and even in her late sixties she was taking donkey trips in the Sierras with her friends.

Characteristically, she suggested to a friend that they walk home from a New York City concert on the day that turned out to be the last one of her life. "Let's walk home," the friend remembered her saying. "The air feels so good."[15]

When her funeral was held at St. Bartholomew's Episcopal Church in New York City in 1944, Herbert Hoover asked that the front pews of the church be reserved not for the celebrities and heads of state who came to mourn his remarkable wife but for her beloved Girl Scouts. Waves of girls in uniforms created a sea of green. No tribute could have brought her more joy.

Lou's interest in outdoor sports began at an early age. The Henrys still lived in Waterloo when this picture was taken— probably shortly before her tenth birthday in 1884.

Chapter 3 ❧ Lou Henry Hoover and Women's Sports

Jan Beran

Lou Henry Hoover's involvement in the Girl Scout movement is well known, but few are aware of her parallel interest in another organization that was equally committed to outdoor recreation and sports. During the 1920s and 1930s, her passion, dedication, organizational skills, and vast network of friends were a propelling force behind the remarkable evolution of a fledgling organization, the Women's Division of the National Amateur Athletic Federation (NAAF), into a major force in the promotion of women's athletics and sport.

Lou was associated with the Women's Division from its inception in 1923 until its merger with the American Association of Physical Education and Recreation in 1940. Her leadership during the formative years and continued financial support were central in the Women's Division efforts to promote "a sport for every girl and every girl in a sport."

Lou was the only female vice president of the NAAF when it was organized in 1922. She advocated a separate division for women because "there was a different ideology of standards and purposes for women's sport."[1] Throughout her life Lou had been active in sport and recreational activities so it was natural for her to commit her energies and remarkable leadership skills to providing and promoting women's athletics.

Lou's childhood in Iowa was a departure from the standard Victorian upbringing of female children in the 1870s. By the time she was six years old, her father had taken her fishing, trapping, hiking, and overnight camping. Those outdoor activities expanded after the family moved to California. She played with both boys and girls in the usual childhood games and enjoyed roller skating, baseball, tennis, horseback riding, and biking.

As a university student Lou focused her energy on her studies, but athletics ranked a close second. She loved the gymnasium where she and other students in dark blue serge middy blouses and bloomers marched, did drills with Indian clubs, dumbbells, and wands, performed on the trapeze, and did tumbling exercises. But she liked sports best, and in daily letters home Lou described her enjoyment of baseball, tennis, archery, basketball, biking, hunting, and fishing. She was a Stanford student when the university started its basketball program and was a member of Stanford's basketball committee in 1896 when Stanford played Berkeley in the first intercollegiate women's basketball game in the United States. In her senior year she was president of the Stanford Women's Athletic Association.

She maintained an active lifestyle during her years in China, London, and Washington, D.C. by hiking, bicycling, playing tennis, and camping. Even in her sixties, she and three friends spent several weeks exploring Oregon's Cascade Mountains on horseback. Throughout their marriage, the Hoovers experienced joy and companionship in outdoor athletic activities. From her family she had first learned to love nature and adventure in the outdoors, to exercise self-reliance, and to be courageous. It was these same values that drew her to the Girl Scout movement.

When the Hoovers returned to the United States from Europe in 1917, they were concerned about a breakdown in family life and welfare and a lack of direction among American youth. Lou, in her customary pragmatic approach, systematically evaluated several youth organizations before deciding that the Girl Scouts was the most effective organization in providing girls with a wide range of activities that enriched their lives.

Lou's overriding ambition for the Girl Scout movement and, later, the Woman's Division of the National Amateur Athletic Federation, was to provide opportunities for every girl and woman to be physically active, preferably outdoors. She lamented the fact that so few women and girls knew how to play and were merely spectators. She wanted all girls to experience what a thrill it was "to throw ourselves into play and action and to get from it the refreshment and invigoration of muscles, nerves and spirit."[2]

Lou's philosophy of play centered around the idea that sport and recreation bring a joyous dimension to life and are essential components of physical and mental health. She was firmly committed to the principle that *all* females should have the opportunity to participate in athletics and believed that mass participation was preferable to channeling resources into the training of a small number of superb athletes for competition. To these ends she gave unstintingly of her ability, time and resources from 1923 to 1928 as president of both the Girl Scouts and the Women's Division and continued that involvement on a lesser scale when she became first lady.

From the beginning of her involvement in the NAAF in 1922, it was evident that Lou Henry Hoover had outstanding organizational abilities and vision. The organization of the NAAF had been prompted by the apparent decline in the health and fitness of Americans. The *New York Herald* of March 25, 1923, quoted Mrs. Hoover:

> The World War showed a vast and appalling number of physical defects among the young men of the nation and it follows as a corollary that a large percentage of young women are likewise handicapped. Much of this can be corrected by proper exercise and I believe full opportunity for reasonable physical development should be afforded.[3]

The two major purposes of the NAAF were (1) to serve as a national organization to promote and facilitate sports for Americans of all ages and (2) to formulate a specific program so comprehensive that in time every man, woman and child could be included in recreational sport activities. Finding that play and athletics for men and women were developing differently, the NAAF voted to establish two separate sections, one for boys and one for girls. NAAF Executive Director Elwood Brown noted, "We wanted women from the beginning.... We need a half dozen Mrs. Hoovers."[4]

As the only woman vice president of NAAF, Lou chaired the first national Conference on Athletics and Physical Education for Women and Girls in April 1923. Conference speakers included physical educators and physicians who addressed such concerns as efficiency standards of females, physical capacity of females, and the availability of recreational sport for females. Among the 300 who attended the first conference in 1923 were women physical educators from colleges and high schools from Maryland to California. Many of these teachers were also educational administrators. They all supported the philosophy of providing more opportunities for all girls and women to participate in sport. Lou's care in planning the conference prompted one national leader to remark: "Your contribution has gone a long way to putting us on the map."[5] Others echoed the opinion of Lida Lee Tall who said that it "was the most worthwhile conference [she] attended for 10 years."[6]

Henry Breckinridge, president of the NAAF, praised Lou for spearheading the formation of the Women's Division. "By far the most important development of the past year has been due to Mrs. Herbert Hoover and the able and devoted women who have worked under her leadership. She has started one of the finest pieces of constructive work ever undertaken for girlhood and womanhood of America. I hope the men will live up to the example set for them by Mrs. Hoover."[7] Breckinridge also affirmed the importance of the conference in formulating a united position regarding girls and women's sport. Indeed, Lou Hoover had a pivotal role in the crusade to revamp the organization of girls and women's sports. She was very much aware of the concerns arising from certain practices.

In the early 1920s, educators and physicians were increasingly concerned that the growing emphasis on highly competitive sport for girls and women would lead to training regimens and competitions that were too strenuous and potentially dangerous. Women physical educators were particularly concerned about the participation of women in the Olympics under the jurisdiction of male coaches and the Amateur Athletic Union (AAU). Three leading women's physical education organizations united in 1923 to protest women's varsity sports, the participation of women in the Olympics, and the "take-over" of female athletes by the AAU. These experts deplored the promotion of girls' sports as spectator sports and went on record opposing female participation in the Olympic games.

From a current perspective, it seems ironic that the Women's Division of the National Amateur Athletic Federation would oppose female participation in the Olympics. But they were aware there were few standards to govern the conduct of sports for girls and women and that well-trained, qualified female coaches were in short supply. The NAAF vehemently opposed highly competitive professional athletics for women because women's sports advocates believed that competitive athletics were injurious to health. They also wanted to guard against the exploitation of girls in sports—demanding schedules, time away from school, and the making of money on female sports. They advocated broad participation. In a time of limited resources for sports they preferred to campaign for activity for all rather than just a few highly skilled individuals.

The Women's Division leaders wanted to avoid the male model of athletics, which they regarded as having serious deficiencies, such as an overemphasis on competition and a lack of integrity. They saw the same pattern developing in the conduct of sports for girls and women. Specific unacceptable practices included long trips to athletic contests on school nights, lack of physical examinations, general disregard of participants' well-being, overemphasis on winning and rivalry, long competitive seasons, derogatory comments from spectators, and the involvement of only a small portion of the students in school.

An overarching concern had to do with male coaches, particularly basketball coaches. There were many problems with men coaching girls' teams, but the major factor was that men did not understand the physiology of girls, especially the need to limit play during the first three days of the menstrual period.

Another cause for alarm came from the attention the media was giving to sports. Press and radio coverage expanded rapidly during the 1920s, capturing the imagination of the public and creating in the process many new sport heroes and heroines. Media attention encouraged spectator sports, professional athletes, and commercial exploitation of sports. These trends were a cause of serious concern. Women educators did not want women's athletics to become spectator sports.

The Women's Division (WD) members were a group of highly independent individuals who agreed upon goals but could not agree on ways to achieve those goals. Lou's initial task as head of the Women's Division was to achieve consensus among the members. "We do not need an exhortation on the *importance* of the correct physical development of our girls, nor of the most satisfactory methods for guiding their athletic endeavors," she said; "indeed it is the subject that most of us give the better hours of our lives to. We want to consider problems whose correct solution, we feel, will bring incalculable influence for good to our race—to the girls and women we know, and incidentally to the boys and men about them."[8] After much discussion, she was successful in leading the group to consensus in the development of a suggested model program.

To counteract the prevailing pattern, Lou and her WD colleagues, mostly college physical education teachers, crusaded for a female model of athletics. In that model, sports for girls and women would be completely separate from male sports. Women would administer, coach, and officiate sports and provide opportunity for every girl and woman to participate in quality instructional programs of physical education and a well-run recreational program. Lou and her colleagues argued that women and girls required from sport "greater joy and recreation in wholesome participation than in the intensive competition that aims at championship and records."[9]

Lou did more than lend her name to the organization. From the start of her leadership in 1923 until her resignation in 1928 as active chair, Lou Henry Hoover took an active role as the Women's Division investigated, deliberated, resolved, developed, promoted, advised, and eventually controlled most athletic programs for girls and women from 1923 until the middle 1930s.

In accepting the responsibility of leadership, she was well aware of the significance of the issues involved. She was not deterred by the fact that she was not a physical educator. In the words of the Women's Division executive secretary, Lou was "big enough to command the attention of busy physical educators."[10] She recognized the importance of equal opportunity for girls' programs. In the 1920s, boys and men's sport programs invariably had the first "right" to use the gym and to have the best equipment and the most qualified coaches. Girls and women were virtually shut out of many recreational programs. Although there was a rise in varsity and elite competition for females, principally in small colleges and rural high schools and in industrial and church leagues, the members of the Women's Division did not view these as the right type of activities. Educators and physicians in the Women's Division believed that highly intense competitive sports were not conducive to the health and welfare of American women and girls.

Lou believed in the physical and mental health benefits of play and an active lifestyle. In a speech to the Women's Division, she modestly declared: "I feel I am but a bit of mechanism in a scheme for carrying out your wishes. If the success attends our various deliberations that we wish, I feel that all congratulations and credit must be attended to you."[11] Clearly, she saw herself as a vehicle for professionals to develop policies and foster public support and unity.

Proceeding in a systematic manner, Lou corresponded and consulted with former associates from her university days at Stanford. She also contacted YMCA personnel, leading public school physical educators, officials of the American Physical Education Association, National Playground Association, and military and government officials. Many of these leaders were males and medical doctors as well as physical educators. It was this unique coalition of physical educators, medical doctors, and her own circle of friends, aided by her political and economic position, that enabled the Women's Division to institute precedent-setting policies in girls and women's recreation and sports.

Working groups within the Women's Division formulated policies and goals. By 1931, the official platform of the Women's Division highlighted the major concerns with an appeal for the

> promotion of competition that stresses enjoyment of sport and the development of good sportsmanship and character rather than those types that emphasize the making and breaking of records and the winning of championships for the enjoyment of spectators and for the athletic reputations or commercial advantage of institutions and organizations.[12]

The platform established philosophical goals and standards of conduct for sport programs that supported Lou's belief that sport was an important part of the educational experience. The platform also made a strong argument for an alternative model of athletics for females.

The organization was successful. Gradually at first, and then more rapidly, schools and colleges held play days wherein females of varying abilities participated in a wide variety of sports and games. Freed from the pressure of playing before spectators and playing primarily to win, girls found friendly competition and camaraderie. Intramural and interclass sports along with instructional physical education became more commonplace in schools and colleges. Cities and agencies such as the Girl Scouts, YWCA, and YWHA began providing recreational sport opportunities for females. Lou encouraged women's service organizations such as the Catholic Women's Association, the American Association of University Women (AAUW), and the Women's Federation to develop educational programs emphasizing the importance of an active lifestyle. She also supported the efforts of reformers to draft appropriate legislation.

Although Lou always claimed that she was not a public speaker, she gave numerous speeches to groups such as the Girl Scouts and Republican women, during which she promoted the philosophy of the Women's Division. She made optimal use of the print media in promoting her viewpoints regarding women and sports. Both during the 1923 conference and later, extensive newspaper coverage featured Mrs. Hoover's leadership role in the "new athletic movement."

The *Pittsburgh Sun* credited her impact on public attitudes, observing that "the ideal girl is now that of a sturdy self reliant girl whose skin instead of being alabaster white has the healthy glow that comes from healthy outdoor life."[13] In her foreword to the small book *Play Day—The Spirit of Sport*, published in 1929 by the Girl Scouts, she expressed her belief that play was essential for physical fitness, mental growth, poise, and self-adjustment. She felt the best type of play for older children was athletics that could foster the spirit of play.

Reflecting the philosophy of women physical educators, she pointed out that although athletics were a long established part of schooling, usually only a few students were selected to play while the remainder were left watching on the sidelines. Lamenting the fact that many youth were denied the opportunity of experiencing the exuberance that comes from physical activity and the camaraderie of being a member of a team, she saw the Women's Division as instrumental in expanding opportunities.

Lou believed that girls were just as capable as men "if they knew their fields."[14] She repeatedly denied that certain activities or occupations diminished womanliness. Although these concepts are generally accepted in the 1990s, attitudes were quite different in the 1920s. Most people were shocked by the freedom displayed by young women during the flapper era when they bobbed their hair and raised their hemlines to their knees. Lou commented on this in one of her speeches. She saw nothing wrong with young women wearing comfortable clothing. After all, it allowed them more freedom for physical activity. Lou herself wore practical clothing, including pants for hiking, horseback riding, and mine inspection trips in Australia and China. She was not disturbed, as were some of her contemporaries in Washington society, by the shortened bloomers and loose-fitting middy blouses worn by students in physical education classes. Comfort and function were more important to her than fashion.

Lou was a very successful fund-raiser for the Women's Division. She buttonholed friends and was successful in garnering support. Friends in the Girl Scout movement, Mary Wallace and the wealthy Spelman-Rockefeller family made generous contributions. With the Women's Division administrative committee, she drafted an institutional membership plan whereby schools and agencies from around the country became members by paying at least $5.00 or more. In a 1923 membership solicitation she noted that there is "a growing need for organization and standardization in physical activities for girls and women, a need to unite not only for our own purposes but in order to help the girl or woman who is not now in any educational or recreational institution and is in need of stimulation and leadership."[15]

She personally donated between $300 and $1,500 each year and secured donations from foundations, which enabled the organization to hire an executive secretary. She was instrumental in securing an annual grant from the American Relief Administration (ARA). These donations kept the Women's Division solvent when it was unable to secure large, long-term grants from major foundations.

The Women's Division philosophy and programs were described in a variety of publications and the leaders frequently addressed state and national conventions. Lou worked closely with the executive director and the executive board in working out a student membership and individual membership plan, allowing her personal calling card to be used along with promotional pamphlets. Once her husband was elected president, Lou resigned her position although she continued to give generous financial support to the organization.

By the late 1930s other groups with competing agendas had entered the field and the influence of the Women's Division dwindled. With the grant from the ARA coming to an end in 1939, the Women's Division leader negotiated a merger with the American Association for Health, Physical Education, and Recreation in 1940. Its leadership in the promotion of sport for girls and women is still significant.

During the half century since assimilation, the goals of the Women's Division have been diluted. The most ardent proponents of "sports for all" were no longer the dominant spokespersons for females. As Joan Hult has noted, the organization's leadership had begun to readjust their conception of competition, to reconcile their practices and their rhetoric with the reality of what many girls and women were doing. They continued to work for sport opportunities for all but there was increasing recognition of the validity of competitive varsity athletics. As expected, the leaders of the former NAAF-WD and the leaders of the new association National Section on Women's Athletics often disagreed. Because of these differences, the association did not endorse or condemn such competition.

The former Women's Division is now a major component (National Association for Girls and Women in Sport) of the American Alliance for Health, Physical Education, Recreation and Dance. The leaders of that group worked for the passage of Title

IX of the Educational Amendments Act in the mid-1970s which requires equity in sport for females and males. The association continues to function as a strong advocate of sport for females. Lou Henry Hoover and her colleagues would be pleased by the current high rate of participation among females in high school and collegiate intramural programs. They would also rejoice in the increasing involvement of Americans in outdoor leisure pursuits. However, the 1920s leaders would be puzzled by the intense physical fitness regimes practiced by some females. And there is little doubt that they would be alarmed at the allocation of so much time, money, and expertise to prepare a few females to perform before spectators in highly intense competitive programs. Just as in 1923, they would take exception to long road trips necessitating school absences, male coaches, attention from the media, and overemphasis on winning and rivalry. They would be amazed at the number of Americans who wile away their time watching televised sports when they could be actively participating. As they did seven decades earlier, they would surely speak out regarding sedentary lifestyles.

So it was that a little girl who fished and camped with her father on the banks of an Iowa river in the 1880s matured to become the principal leader in a national organization that fostered increased recreational and sporting activities for all females in the United States. Lou Henry Hoover's passionate advocacy of the right of all individuals to an active outdoors life helped turn a small organization into a national group that included both public and private schools at all levels, religious organizations, youth leagues and organizations, national sports groups, private sport clubs, and industrial sports leagues. The Women's Division's influence eventually assumed international proportions when it played a role in the development of programs in Brazil, Italy, and the Philippines.

Lou Henry Hoover's leadership as president of the Women's Division of the NAAF was all the more remarkable because it was one of many causes to which she was dedicated. Known as a woman with a love of justice, clearness of vision and charming candor, she was efficient, careful with people's feelings, always well prepared, and capable of mastering any emergency.

She was a woman of her time and yet a person ahead of her time. She crusaded for many causes aimed at improving the human condition, but she will be especially remembered for her efforts to promote sports and recreation opportunities for women.

She dedicated much of her energy and time to promote "an aim which is thoroughly American and democratic, . . . to give every girl and boy an equal opportunity for health, an equal opportunity for joyous recreation . . . with a focus on relaxation and fun for all instead of overexertion for a few, bleacher seats for the many and too strained intentness for all."[16]

After retiring from active leadership she wrote, "Already the play day spirit has found a strong foothold . . . the aim of play days is a vital one for America. It has in mind the happiness and success of every individual. This new plan for athletics embodies the spirit of true play."[17]

The First Lady's spontaneous good humor is evident in this candid shot taken during a stopover on a trip to Florida in 1932. She was also an avid fan of home movie taking and kept her camera close at hand.

Chapter 4 ❧ A Neglected First Lady: A Reappraisal of Lou Henry Hoover

Lewis L. Gould

Among the women who have been first ladies since 1900, Lou Henry Hoover has been the most obscure and forgotten. Her successor in the institution was Eleanor Roosevelt, whose restless energy and liberal activism set a historical standard against which all presidential wives have been measured. Even Mrs. Hoover's predecessor, the stylish Grace Coolidge, has eclipsed her in the popular mind. Much like her husband's role as president, Mrs. Hoover's four years in the White House seemed to be the end of the older type of passive first ladies. She has been viewed as only a pause before the arrival of Eleanor Roosevelt and the modern presidential spouse.[1]

In part, Lou Hoover was simply unlucky. After her death in 1944, Herbert Hoover specified that her papers could not be opened for research until twenty years after he died. The former president lived until 1964, which meant that Mrs. Hoover's historical reputation was frozen for more than four decades. Assessments of Mrs. Hoover's performance, even those of recent years, have reflected the verdict that she did not have a large impact as first lady. "Mrs. Hoover selected no major projects or causes, but pursued a number of interests in public silence," wrote Myra Gutin about her. In analyzing Mrs. Hoover's response to the hard times of the American economy, Carl Anthony concluded, "Publicly, however, she became more subdued, steadfastly refusing to publicly acknowledge the total bleakness the Depression was wreaking." Betty Caroli sums up the negative consensus about Mrs. Hoover: "More than most of her predecessors, Lou Hoover had exceptional ability and training for leadership, but she failed to win the country's approval or its interest." Caroli's final verdict is devastating. "While she set the stage for Eleanor's accomplishments, she came nowhere close to equalling them."2

When Mrs. Hoover's papers are investigated more thoroughly, researchers will discover a more complex woman whose involvement with the issues of the time was greater than has been previously understood. Lou Hoover did make important contributions to the institution of the first lady, several of which anticipate Eleanor Roosevelt's subsequent actions. During the Great Depression, moreover, she used her favorite cause, the Girl Scouts, as a means of marshaling public support behind her husband's policies. In that effort, she showed herself willing to use the influence of her position with a great deal of adroitness and energy. Measured in the context of the historical development of the unique role of the first lady in American political and cultural life, Lou Henry Hoover deserves to be seen as a significant figure among modern presidential wives. Even her failures and false starts are instructive for they reveal the limits on the first lady's activities during the early years of this century.

One common observation about Mrs. Hoover concerns her "reticence" as first lady compared with the more outgoing style of Eleanor Roosevelt. Mrs. Hoover's papers indicate that the exact nature of her "reticence" must be reappraised. From the outset of her husband's presidency, the first lady used the radio as a means of reaching the public. Her reliance on this new medium of communication predates the Depression. She had spoken on the radio before her husband became president, but did not do so after his inauguration until April 19, 1929. Then she made "a brief address" when the Daughters of the American Revolution dedicated Constitution Hall in Washington. She made only a few remarks in her "gracious little speech," but the occasion represented "the first time in history that the voice of a First Lady was heard over the radio."[3]

In May 1929 the Secretary of Agriculture Arthur M. Hyde asked her to "speak briefly" over the National Broadcasting Company to the Third National 4-H Club Camp Meeting on the grounds of the Agriculture Department. Mrs. Hoover responded that she "should love to do it" if arrangements could be made to produce the broadcast to fit her husband's schedule. That proved no problem at all for the technicians of the Radio Corporation of America, and on June 22, 1929, she gave her "informal talk" from the Hoover's weekend camp in the Virginia mountains.[4]

Mrs. Hoover's twenty-minute speech was much longer than the one she had delivered to the DAR. The 4-H experiences, she said, were training the boys and girls "to meet the larger demands of the future upon you." She told them in conclusion: "Girls and boys studying the problems of farming and *home* making! What a wonderful combination that is." The theme of using youthful experiences to meet the social responsibilities of the nation was one that Mrs. Hoover would raise in future broadcasts.[5]

When the severity of the Depression became apparent in 1931, Mrs. Hoover adapted her radio appearances to rally support for her husband's programs to alleviate the impact of hard times. She spoke several times during the year on that subject. She gave a radio broadcast on March 23, 1931 on behalf of the Women's Division of the President's Emergency Committee for Employment (PECE), during which she discussed the role of the Girl Scouts in pursuing volunteer campaigns to relieve the depression. On May 6, 1931, she addressed another nationwide audience at a Mother's Day Luncheon given by the Maternity Center Association in New York City. Finally, on November 7, 1931, she again spoke nationally to the 4-H Clubs and told her listeners, "There is something for each one of you to do in this emergency—a special achievement awaiting you."[6]

Mrs. Hoover took her public appearances seriously. When she had difficulty making herself heard at one occasion, she arranged to have "a small, improvised laboratory" established on the second floor of the White House. Reporters noted that she was "seeking a method of speech and intonation that would make her voice record better." The news story, however, irritated the first lady and the use of the laboratory was canceled. The White House staff questioned reporters about the source of the leak.[7]

Following her husband's defeat in the 1932 presidential election, Mrs. Hoover made a final radio address for the National Women's Committee of the Welfare and Relief Mobilization of 1932 on November 27, 1932. Speaking on "The Woman's Place in the Present Emergency," she told women that "one of our most important duties is to find when, how and where are the people to be helped." She urged them to become "unofficial Associated Members" of the relief agencies in their communities and help those bodies "find and chart the needs of those who most deserve assistance." She suggested that women might find useful volunteer roles in hospitals and as teachers of young children who would otherwise be neglected during the Depression. It was time, the first lady said, "to give not only a helping hand, but a willing ear and an understanding heart to those in little or in great need about us."[8]

Mrs. Hoover's use of the radio to communicate her views on the Depression was her method of promoting the president's position that volunteerism and individual initiative, rather than government relief programs, were preferable responses to the economic distress. Her activism on behalf of this conservative position has not commended itself to historians of the institution of the first lady. Yet in practice it is hard to distinguish between Mrs.

Hoover's use of the mass media in this way and similar techniques that Eleanor Roosevelt adopted during the 1930s.

The general topic of Mrs. Hoover's press relations should also be reopened both in light of her radio campaigns and her handling of the press in another respect. The usual interpretation is that Mrs. Hoover cut herself off from the press and declined to give interviews. "As First Lady," says Myra Gutin, "Lou Hoover refused to grant interviews or to be quoted." In practice, however, the process was less structured and restrictive than that. For example, during a visit to New York in September 1929 to open a benefit exhibition for the Girl Scouts, the first lady "talked informally for about ten minutes to the news writers." Mrs. Hoover sat on a Queen Anne chair, "and the news writers arranged themselves, sitting on the floor cross-legged, in Girl Scout fashion, around the First Lady of the Land."[9]

A year later, during another visit to New York, Mrs. Hoover "saw reporters informally, but declined to be interviewed." By 1932, reporters were referring to her "annual interview" that dealt with Girl Scout matters. The ground rules were that Mrs. Hoover "received newspaper reporters with the stipulation that their questions must concern Girl Scout work." Because the first lady used the Girl Scouts to push the administration's programs to defeat the Depression, the practical effect was to give a wider scope for reporters' inquiries than the apparent ban on interviews would suggest.[10]

The papers of Mrs. Hoover are also revealing in regard to the most famous incident of her tenure in the White House: the luncheon attended by the wife of black Congressman Oscar DePriest in June 1929. The papers illuminate this episode's affect on the relations of the Hoover administration with Southern Democrats and African-Americans within the Republican party. The letters that Mrs. Hoover received about her hospitality to Mrs. DePriest also indicate much about popular attitudes toward the role of the first lady at the end of the 1920s.

Although Mrs. Hoover's papers do not shed light on the motives behind the decision to invite Mrs. DePriest to have tea at the White House on June 12, 1929, they do indicate the care with which the first lady and her secretary, Mary Randolph, approached the arrangements for the occasion. The election of Oscar DePriest from a Chicago district in 1928 posed the question of how his wife should be treated when the wives of House and Senate members had their annual tea party at the White House. Not wishing to risk a public snub from southerners if all the wives came to one event, and unwilling to cancel the tea tradition altogether, the Hoovers decided on four separate teas, with Mrs. DePriest coming to the last one. In that way, the other women in attendance would be screened to minimize the possibility of an embarrassing incident.[11]

The guest lists for the tea parties on June 4, 1929, and June 12, 1929, were carefully gone over to produce a small group of women in which Mrs. DePriest would be treated politely. There were fourteen women present, including Mrs. Hoover, her secretaries Ruth Fesler and Mary Randolph, and the wives of the attorney general and the secretary of war. The White House also took pains to keep the invitation as quiet as possible. Sending the invitation to Mrs. DePriest, Mary Randolph instructed the White House messenger to keep the matter "confidential and caution messenger to refrain from giving information regarding it." The afternoon went off very smoothly, but news of the event soon became public. Congressman DePriest said his wife "was treated excellently, and there was no indication of a desire to discriminate in her case. Naturally, she is very pleased with the whole affair." A storm of protest from Southern Democrats soon ensued.[12]

The DePriest episode occurred in a volatile political setting. President Hoover had carried five southern states against Al Smith in the 1928 election, and the Republicans had hopes of breaking the Democratic monopoly in the "solid South." On that score, the White House was reluctant to offend the racial sensibilities of the white South. However, the president was also concerned to indicate to African-Americans that there was a place for them in the Republican party. Moreover, both of the Hoovers had a more inclusive and tolerant view of blacks in 1929 than the majority of their fellow citizens. The Hoover's had refused to sign a restrictive covenant when they purchased their S Street house because it would have barred its rental to either Jews or blacks. Mrs. Hoover also extended private acts of charity to her black servants, including a willingness to fund a college education for one of her maids. Mrs. Hoover and her husband talked over the question of inviting Mrs. DePriest, and concluded that it was the kind of appropriate gesture they could make toward encouraging black progress.[13]

The public announcement that the tea party had occurred and that Mrs. DePriest had been to the White House brought a flood of mail to the first lady praising and criticizing what she had done. "The burden of mail became so great," noted one of Mrs. Hoover's secretaries, that the task of responding to it was shifted to President Hoover's aides. From a political point of view, the most significant response came in the form of resolutions denouncing Mrs. Hoover that were introduced and passed in several southern state legislatures. The most inflammatory was the one from Texas that proclaimed that southerners would never "condone any act or conduct that would tend in the least to sanction social racial equality as between the white and negro races." In part, the resolution was a political move by Texas Democrats to rally their party after losing the state to Hoover and the Republicans a year earlier. It also reflected the extent to which racial segregation was still a fundamental part of the creed of white Democrats in Texas.[14]

Many of those who wrote Mrs. Hoover endorsed her invitation to Mrs. DePriest. Mary Austin, the southwestern writer, commended the first lady for "treating the color prejudice exactly as it deserves to be treated: the ghost of an ancient and un-American error." The editor of a hardware journal in Kansas City wrote, "You and your estimable husband have shown the true spirit of America." The Colored Women's Auxiliary of the Martha Washington Republican Women's Club of Buffalo, New York, wired, "You have set a precedent of American ideals and principles that we hope will be followed by all True Americans."[15]

The feelings of other whites, North and South, about the first lady's gesture was vehement outrage at the breach of segregation and racial lines. "Social equality between the races is unthinkable and would ruin the country," wrote a Pennsylvania woman. A Texas man added "that kind of treatment of the negro does not set well with those of the southland, who love the negro in his place, but not at our dinner table." A Virginia Democrat sent a gleeful telegram to Mrs. Hoover: "Your social equality tea will go a long way towards rallying the shattered ranks of democracy in the solid South. Thank you. Have another."[16]

Mrs. Hoover did not repeat the DePriest episode. Her biographer noted that the first lady became "a little more reserved in her manner toward reporters." Lacking the sense for the right public gesture that Eleanor Roosevelt possessed, Mrs. Hoover did not affirm publicly the basis for her invitation to Mrs. DePriest nor take the opportunity to assert the principal of equality before the law. Instead, she deferred to the political considerations that animated her husband and his aides in dealing with the volatile race problem.[17]

The overriding political and economic problem for the Hoovers after 1929, of course, was the Great Depression. Assessments of Mrs. Hoover's response to the hardship and suffering of that period have generally been critical or unfavorable. Like the president, Mrs. Hoover approached the issue of providing relief to the unemployed and poor based on her previous experience with voluntary organizations. In her case that meant the Girl Scouts.

Soon after the Crash she began to receive appeals for help from families in distress. Hundreds of these requests were received during the last two months of 1929 and many more appeals were received in 1930. Turning to her vast circle of friends, Mrs. Hoover tried to find a local source of assistance for every appeal, referring cases to individuals, local welfare organizations and local chapters

of national organizations such as the American Red Cross, the
Parent Teachers Association, the General Federation of Women's
Clubs, and the American Friends Service Committee. In some
cases, when no local source of assistance was available, she
provided help anonymously.

By the spring of 1931 it was obvious that she and her social
secretary would be unable to cope with the ever increasing number
of appeals so Mrs. Hoover hired another part-time secretary. She
also realized that she would need to enlist more volunteers. Her
speeches that spring and summer reveal that she was drifting to the
realization that only one organization could provide such a large
number of volunteers—the Girl Scouts.

Mrs. Hoover's work with the Girl Scouts has long been recognized as the most significant contribution of her life. Scholars are
just now beginning to examine the first lady's role in this organization that played such a large part in socializing young women in
the United States after its founding in 1912. The Lou Hoover
papers contain an abundance of materials on the internal work-
ings of the Girl Scouts. In the middle 1920s, Mrs. Hoover had
taken the lead in financing the expansion of the Girl Scout
program. In 1929 and 1930, for example, Mrs. Hoover was deeply
concerned about reorganization and fund-raising plans for the
Girl Scouts, and she participated in negotiations that led to
changes in the leadership of the group with the resignation of Jane
Deeter Rippin, the long-time executive director. A salient issue for
Mrs. Hoover in these discussions was her belief in "the advantages
of a democracy in Girl Scouting, both theoretically and practically,
over an aristocracy, an oligarchy, or a bureaucracy."[18]

To succeed Rippin in the spring of 1930, Mrs. Hoover pushed
hard for a friend she had known for many years: Lillian M.
Gilbreth. Mrs. Hoover described Gilbreth as "one who gets much
accomplished." That was a typical understatement. In fact, Lillian
Gilbreth was one of the more interesting women of the time. With
her husband, Frank Gilbreth, an industrial engineer, she became
a leader in the field of technological efficiency through the

application of time and motion studies to the workplace. Following her husband's death in 1924, Gilbreth shifted her focus toward the use of her methods in the home. She wrote *The Homemaker and Her Job* (1927) and taught at Purdue University. The Gilbreths had twelve children, and their child-rearing exploits were later recorded in the best-selling book which was written by two of their children,[19] *Cheaper by the Dozen* (1948).

Mrs. Hoover's campaign on behalf of Lillian Gilbreth did not succeed, but Gilbreth did conduct a study for the Girl Scouts on "the use of space" at the National Headquarters during June 1930. Meanwhile, Gilbreth served on President Hoover's Committee on Housing and was named to the President's Emergency Committee for Employment when that informal body was created in 1930 under the leadership of Colonel Arthur Woods. The committee, known as PECE, reflected President Hoover's strong conviction that the effects of the economic downturn could best be met through the cooperative efforts of voluntary relief agencies.[20]

The first lady shared her husband's faith in this approach, and she envisioned the Girl Scouts as a means to demonstrate the value of enlightened voluntarism during the Depression. As members of a national organization, the Girl Scouts could be a presence in all communities without intruding or presenting themselves as direct agents of the national government in Washington. Genevieve Brady, a national Girl Scout leader, reported to Mrs. Hoover in January 1931 that "the girls all through the country have been trying to help in the unemployment crisis. Some have been donating their weekly dues for the purchase of milk for babies, bread for the breadlines and general supplies for needy families." Brady asked the first lady to recognize these efforts by meeting with some local Girl Scouts from Washington. "It would mean so much to think you appreciated their idea of service in this national crisis."[21]

Mrs. Hoover then began documenting the activities of Girl Scouts across the country. She arranged to give a nationwide radio address on March 23, 1931 as part of the work of a program about the work of the Women's Division of PECE. In her remarks, she noted that the Girl Scouts represented "the girls and women of the country, in meeting and to a large degree overcoming the threatening disaster of the national situation." She emphasized "the value of the widely flung national organization" that could take "from the still-supplied outstretched hand of the giving on one side, and place its largesse in the empty-hand out-stretched for receiving on the other side." The chairman of the committee, Arthur Woods, wrote her that "the picture you gave of general cooperation was most stimulating."[22]

During the spring and summer of 1931, Mrs. Hoover used several occasions to repeat her ideas about mutual aid among Americans. At the May 6, 1931, meeting in New York for the Maternity Center Association, she praised the group for being ready "to give a helping hand whenever it is asked throughout the country." In late August, the president of the General Federation of Women's Clubs reported to the press after a conference with the first lady at the White House that Mrs. Hoover's plans to deal with the Depression included "organized social groups marshaling forces to meet the emergencies which may arise during the coming months in an effort to prevent want from lack of employment or other causes, just as we met emergencies in the years of the war."[23]

The Girl Scouts remained the focus of Mrs. Hoover's attention. With the organization's annual convention scheduled for Buffalo, New York, in October, she invited the members of the Executive Committee of the Girl Scouts to meet with her at the presidential retreat at Rapidan Camp on September 23. One of the invited guests who could not be present wired Mrs. Hoover that she had wanted to attend "the meeting which must open a new epoch for Girl Scouting." The gathering did just that. Under Mrs. Hoover's leadership, the participants reviewed "the whole economic and relief-demanding situation of our country" with special attention to how "girls of Scout age" might then "be of service." With Lillian Gilbreth's "practical experience in industrial and economic affairs," the Executive Committee produced an outline for "the

Girl Scout program for this period of depression." The Rapidan Plan, as it was called, envisioned that 250,000 Girl Scouts nationally become involved in voluntary relief work.[24]

At the Buffalo convention, Genevieve Brady, president of the organization, gave her report on "Depression Activities for Girl Scouts." However, no explicit provision had been made for Lillian Gilbreth to take part in the convention, at that point. Mrs. Hoover wired the leaders of the meeting before her arrival: "Is Dr. Gilbreth not going to appear before the assembled delegates and lead a little discussion whose start has been pre-arranged?" As a result of Mrs. Hoover's request, Gilbreth then guided the Rapidan Plan to adoption by the entire convention.[25]

Mrs. Hoover envisioned the Rapidan Plan as a model that all women could follow. She suggested in a national radio address from Buffalo that "the one who is not in trouble will have to help the one who is in trouble." She had Lillian Gilbreth carry her message back to Washington. Shortly after the Buffalo meeting, Gilbreth saw Walter Gifford, who had succeeded Arthur Woods as chairman of what was now called the President's Organization on Unemployment Relief (POUR). She told him "of Girl Scouts' willingness to help," and reported "that all will be provided for." Gilbreth also discussed with the Women's Auxiliary of the American Society of Mechanical Engineers how to create "a plan of cooperation" with POUR "as the Girl Scouts are doing, emphasizing specially the needs of keeping engineering students in schools and colleges." In the case of both the Girl Scouts and the engineering women, the first lady wanted to persuade young people not to leave school at a time when jobs were scarce. Mrs. Hoover hosted the engineering auxiliary on December 9, 1931; her tea provided what Gilbreth called "the impetus for a good conference—and it went off smoothly."[26]

Mrs. Hoover also carried her message of voluntarism in relief to the 4-H clubs in her radio broadcast of November 7: Youthful listeners who lived in areas that had "no actual want" should "help plan that the excess in your community may be systematically gathered together and through the aid of the many channels for relief may be sent where it is needed." She urged her audience to "plan how *you* may help those who want desperately to help themselves, but can find no practical way to do so."[27]

How extensively the Rapidan Plan was implemented during 1932 is still not clear. Mrs. Hoover had few doubts of its effectiveness. Looking back on her relief campaign a year later, Mrs. Hoover told the annual Girl Scout convention in October 1932, "The effort has had the natural impetus of the girls themselves— with the restrained advice of their Leaders." The scouts had assisted with relief for children in orphanages while some troops had "specialized in helping old people." She was pleased to report that "Girl Scout groups are increasingly being asked to participate in plans for relief and recreation this winter" that would in turn "be better coordinated with other services being done in the community."[28]

By October 1932, the Hoover presidency was in deep political trouble because the Depression had worsened as the presidential election neared. Despite her husband's impending defeat, Mrs. Hoover continued her work to mobilize women as volunteers in a nongovernmental relief campaign along the lines that she had promoted with the Girl Scouts. She gave her last radio address as first lady on November 27, 1932, on behalf of the National Women's Committee of the Welfare and Relief Mobilization of 1932. The proposal sounded like an expanded version of the Rapidan initiative. The chair of the women's committee was Genevieve Brady of the Girl Scouts and the task of the mobilization itself was to provide help "with energetic support" to "all of the welfare and relief agencies of the country." The larger aim was to serve as "a central clearing house for information on how, where and when people can help."[29]

Like her husband, Mrs. Hoover saw only a small role for government in the process of providing relief to the unemployed and destitute during the Depression. Her voluntaristic vision has come to seem irrelevant before the sheer scale of the economic problem that the downturn of the early 1930s posed. In that sense, her work with the Girl Scouts may seem like only a sidelight to the larger failure of the Hoover administration to cope with the economic crisis facing the nation. The distress that the American people confronted in 1931 and 1932 was far too great for the meager resources of the Girl Scouts, for all their dedication.

In the perspective of the role of the first lady, however, Mrs. Hoover's private campaign and her efforts to utilize the Girl Scouts gains in importance. It represented a concerted and sustained attempt by the president's wife to intervene personally and to use her influence to promote her husband's programs and goals. Although first ladies had addressed serious issues before (Ellen Wilson voiced concerns about living conditions in Washington; Florence Harding opposed cruelty to animals; and Grace Coolidge championed the education of the deaf), Mrs. Hoover took the cause—Girl Scouting—with which she had long been identified and broadened it in response to the Depression.

Her enlistment of Lillian Gilbreth as part of the relief program that she developed for the Girl Scouts was an innovative use of outside experts to assist the first lady in her work. Mrs. Hoover used women she knew through Girl Scouting as an informal network to provide direct assistance to needy families and to expand that network tremendously by utilizing local Girl Scout troops. Although this network depended upon the efforts of well-connected and wealthy women who shared Mrs. Hoover's conservative ideas, it resembled the more liberal networks that Eleanor Roosevelt was building within the Democratic party during the same period. The role of Mrs. Hoover in the area of voluntaristic relief during the Depression merits more examination and analysis than it has previously received.

Her years as first lady also deserve extensive scrutiny. She traveled a great deal and was very much in the public eye during her four years in Washington. The radio broadcasts that she gave set a precedent for what Eleanor Roosevelt would do after her. Although Mrs. Hoover's relations with the press are usually depicted as troubled, a closer look at what she did reveals a more fruitful relationship with the media.

The Hoovers did not turn the DePriest episode into an affirmation of racial equality, but in fairness it should be noted that in 1929 Franklin D. Roosevelt as governor of New York denied that he had invited African-Americans to dine with him in Albany. Also, it was later revealed that the Roosevelts had not objected to a restrictive covenant in the deed to their house in Warm Springs, Georgia. In comparing Mrs. Hoover's actions in the DePriest case with Eleanor Roosevelt's response to the barring of Marian Anderson from Constitutional Hall in 1939, it is also appropriate to note the passage of a decade in which racial attitudes had begun to change and that the participation of black voters in the Democratic party had been welcomed.

Lou Henry Hoover's record as first lady thus was more complex than the customary picture of docile inactivity that is so often contrasted with the energy and commitment of Eleanor Roosevelt. Mrs. Hoover traveled extensively, as did Mrs. Roosevelt. Mrs. Hoover used the emerging technology of radio to spread her views. So too did Eleanor Roosevelt. Mrs. Hoover exerted her influence on behalf of her husband's programs and saw herself as an arm of the presidential administration in its response to the challenges of the Depression just as Mrs. Roosevelt would later do. Though they were two very different women in their personal styles and public appeal, there were also important elements of continuity between Lou Henry Hoover and Eleanor Roosevelt that deserve greater attention from scholars than they have received. In that sense, as in others, Lou Henry Hoover was an important figure in the history of the institution of the first lady who should be better remembered than she is.

Mrs. Hoover was very interested in preserving the history of the White House and its traditions. The desk at which she is seated is an exact replica of the desk at which President Monroe wrote the famous Monroe Doctrine.

Chapter 5 ❧ Lou Henry Hoover and the White House

William Seale

The White House that received Lou Henry Hoover and the new president on March 4, 1929, was in its essentials the house George Washington had built in the 1790s. Relatively minor alterations over the years had culminated twenty-seven years before, in 1902, in a major remodeling by Theodore Roosevelt, who directed the celebrated New York architectural firm McKim, Mead & White to preserve the historical character of the residence, but make it into a modern working headquarters for the chief of state. The lofty, snowy white hall that Lou Hoover entered as first lady, with its pairs of heavy plaster columns and hard stone floors was Roosevelt's; his also were the elegantly cosmopolitan state rooms that brimmed with silks and reproduction European-style furniture, settings as dated as one could imagine, but of a type the president's wife had known as high-style when she lived in England.

She was the first of her type of first lady. There had been activists before. Caroline Harrison, who, between going to the White House in 1889 and her death there in 1892, worked in women's organizations, teaching the newly formed Daughters of the American Revolution how to win in politics. Ellen Axson

Wilson, first wife of Woodrow Wilson, spent her few years in the White House seeking the improvement of living conditions for black renters in Washington's shameful alley slums. If Lou Hoover followed in any tradition it was theirs; but she sought more. Her predecessor, Grace Goodhue Coolidge, had been the first who might be called a media star. The glamour of the 1920s White House was hers, and she gave the nation a beautiful first lady, who was a model of strength in the loss of her teenage son and always a woman Americans were proud to see. She was the president's wife, a woman somewhat astonished by the public attention that was showered on her and really liking it, whether President Coolidge did or not. Mrs. Hoover, more than earlier women of the White House, saw in her position an opportunity to broadcast principles she believed in, especially about how women should prepare themselves to take a more integral part in the shaping of American life.

The Hoovers went to the White House in what was considered a golden age of prosperity. Economic indicators predicted even better times. Herbert Hoover was the most highly respected humanitarian in the United States. It was widely known that the Hoovers had made their fortune in mining, and then retired to give service to the world. Herbert Hoover's was a brilliant American success story, crowned with the distinction of the presidency. His leadership in the feeding and recovery of a vanquished Europe seemed to elevate him to a level above mere politics, and the independent, activist tone of the man was part of his appeal as a presidential candidate. He had emerged unblemished from the cabinet scandals that followed President Warren G. Harding's death in office and had continued under Calvin Coolidge as secretary of commerce. Herbert Hoover was known for his strong character and astute business sense. His square-jawed book *American Individualism* is a sort of poetry for the iridescent 1920s, celebrating the promise of American idealism contrasted with the failure of Europe's reactionary political chauvinism.

Herbert and Lou Hoover were, in terms of personal spending

power, the richest couple to live in the White House since Rutherford B. Hayes and would be until the 1960s. It was a well-managed, self-made fortune, and Hoover's business ability had not diminished. As still relatively young people, the Hoovers had become wealthy and accustomed to a style of living that was more than comfortable. At various houses in which they had lived all over the world they maintained large staffs of servants and entertained extensively. In England they had a London house and a country estate, living between the two and conducting an extensive social life. It was in the intellectual climate of these high British circles that Mrs. Hoover first saw herself as an instrument for the realization of humanitarian ideals. Perhaps responding to the confusion and decline of the prewar feminist movement after World War I, she turned her interest by the 1920s to the improvement of women and the modernizing of their attitudes about their own roles in the world. If Mrs. Hoover can be pegged with any single word that describes her ideals it is "modernist."

When she became first lady, Lou Henry Hoover was fifty-four, several months older than the president. Her hair was white, coiffed in a smart marcel. A conservative dresser, she photographed rather motherly but was considered a very handsome woman. She took vigorous physical exercise and loved it, so, although she was overweight, she kept herself fit and wore good clothes nicely. Like Helen Taft before her, she had gained a taste for rich silks, fine linen, and colorful printed cotton in the Orient. Formal occasions at the White House still demanded court trains for the principal ladies, and Mrs. Hoover made a very grand appearance in yards and yards of embroidered silks and jewelry Herbert Hoover had given her. An informal photograph taken of her in the White House rose garden in 1929 shows her with her German shepherd in a dress that might be of linen; it is white, with dark embroidery at the top, an open collar, and long sleeves; a large straw handbag is over her arm. Around her neck and hanging on a chain to her waist are lorgnettes, for she allowed herself the vanity of restricting the use of regular glasses to private times.

The staff of the Hoover White House was part new and part inherited, which had been the tradition. (Today the household employees are almost entirely inherited from previous administrations.) When the Hoovers moved in the existing White House domestic staff of some thirty employees included about two-thirds servants and the rest functionaries of various kinds, including the venerable Ike Hoover, the chief usher, who presided over all. Personal servants came with the Hoovers. If the mingling was tranquil, it was the first and last in the history of the place. It would be some weeks before the White House staff learned to accommodate the Hoovers and before the Hoovers learned that there were many White House ways of doing things that were perpetuated simply because they worked no matter how odd they might seem to outsiders.

Thanks to the Coolidges, the White House was a more comfortable house than it had ever been. In 1927 President Coolidge permitted the replacement of the old wood-framed attic with a third floor framed in steel beneath a new larger and steeper roof silhouette. As the basement served the state floor with auxiliary rooms, so the new third floor served the second floor family quarters with service rooms and servants and guests' quarters. Herbert and Lou Hoover occupied the traditional presidential bedroom and dressing room on the southwest corner of the second floor. Outside their door was the sitting room at the end of the west hall, with its giant half-moon window that looked out on brilliant sunsets over and around the sharp Parisian roof outlines of the State, War and Navy Building.

If the Hoovers walked briskly through the front door that first day, it can be said that their pace was not broken for seven months thereafter. They were the busiest of people, and both were very social. Dinners, parties of all kinds, meetings, and excursions away from home characterized nearly every waking hour that was not consumed by work; for they worked as they played. White House traditions were carefully observed, but entertaining had a long tradition in the family. Mrs. Hoover, president of the Girl Scouts of America, put the *Girl Scout Handbook* on the social desk as one of the references for procedures.

Never before in the history of the White House had there been as extensively staffed and as busy a social branch of the operation. There was little difference in the character of the White House parties, for the Hoovers had known these for many years and appreciated the traditions, but the guest lists were longer. And the food was better, the kitchen budget supplemented from the president's own purse. Privately the Hoovers treated themselves at the White House rather as guests. They ate every dinner in the State Dining Room, he in dinner suit, she in long dress; this custom was followed even when there was no company, though there was nearly always company. By long White House tradition, guests were classed in three unspoken categories: official guests, personal friends and family, and the "made list," which identified members of Washington society. This last was a long list of local people who were considered suitable—and safe in point of behavior—to fill out White House entertainments.

Since 1800, when John Adams became the first president to occupy the White House, Washington society circulated around the "season" at the White House, December to February. In Lou Hoover's time, the season extended to the garden parties in May. She loved every facet of the season. Resident with her husband in Europe, England, and the Orient, she had become well known as an accomplished hostess, and the White House was an extension of years of experience giving teas, dinners, dances, presentations, and house parties. She insisted upon having a large staff, for she managed people well and was very particular in the delegation of responsibility; her husband ran his business the same way. The White House domestic payroll increased by about 20 percent, although it varied over the four years.

Tradition gave sheen to the elegant social performance. Coolidge had hesitated at the age-old custom of the president marching into an entertainment to music. Hoover, hesitating not at all, had the Marine Band roll the drums and strike up "Hail to the Chief" while he and Mrs. Hoover and their special guests descended the grand stair. The Hoovers stood in the Blue Room to receive guests, while their house party posed in the south ends of the Blue, Green, and Red rooms, behind velvet ropes. At great receptions long receiving lines poured thousands of guests into the East Room. When the line was ended, the Hoovers walked into the East Room and stood beneath the central chandelier. Young military aides—called social aides—brought specific guests forward to stand and talk to the president and first lady. When the "Blue Danube Waltz" was played, the Hoovers turned and left the room, ascending the grand stair to the second floor. Sometimes dancing followed in the East Room for about an hour, but usually the president's departure was the signal that the event was over.

For all their adherence to formality, the Hoovers found that they could not please the State Department all the time. Although they respected their positions, they were not in themselves formal people and sometimes took precedence of rank lightly. A major controversy centered around the White House status of Mrs. Edward E. Gann, half-sister of the vice president, Charles Curtis. Since the death of Mrs. Curtis, Dolly Gann had been his hostess, and thus believed that she deserved the rank of vice president's wife at official Washington dinner tables. At private parties this was duly accorded, if occasionally with a wink. Not so when at last the issue was tested at the White House. The State Department, which held supreme power over White House protocol, refused to give her a place at the table where the vice president's wife traditionally sat, and Mrs. Gann's protests were so loud as to push the embroilment into the press, where she appeared front page nation-wide. Many congressional wives, who felt that the flamboyant Dolly was an upstart, took delight in the controversy. Ultimately Dolly Gann was silenced by being given her way, but not without embarrassment such a seemingly foolish dispute would bring on any house, much less the White House. Lou Hoover wisely stayed clear of "Dolly Gann's War."

The coming of the Depression in the autumn of 1929 slowed the pace of entertainment for the Hoovers, as they watched the economic situation worsen. In hindsight, it is clear that the old way of doing things at the White House was over. There would still be receptions and dinners, ceremonies and musicales, but as part of the official routine, not in a social whirl. Mrs. Hoover was not one to close down. She held children's parties and special events for organizations, for she dearly loved volunteer organizations. Her emphasis upon this, too, reflected the president's challenge to the nation to revive the volunteer spirit of old in helping pull the economy out of the Depression.

Choirs sang in the East Room. Teas were held for a thousand or more weekly, featuring this or that special group, including many women's organizations. Mrs. Hoover stood up and spoke to her guests, cheering them and encouraging them. She was a popular first lady and her limited public comments were widely reported. Often repeated was her ardent belief that women should be activist, pursuing sports and self-education, and entering into all aspects of American life. She did not see women as deprived, but as reluctant to fulfill themselves.

Her strong feelings against bigotry surfaced when she entertained Mrs. Oscar DePriest, wife of a black congressman from Chicago, at a White House tea for congressional wives. The sensitivity of the event must be seen in the context of a segregated capital. Careful planning went into the reception that Mrs. DePriest attended to avoid any incident that would embarrass her or the White House. This seems odd in a modern context, but it was radical in an era in which political society also rejected Mormons, whom Mrs. Hoover also received, and others in a strange scale of values. The first lady suffered harsh criticism, to the extent that she feared she had done damage to her husband's career.

The year 1929 began with a boom for the Hoovers and ended in one disappointment after another. In the shadow of the Great

Depression's early months, they held a Christmas Eve dinner for family and key staff members at the White House. Suddenly the West Wing, which had just been remodeled, caught fire and burned. A water-soaked rug was thrown over the president's desk in the Oval Office to protect it, while secret papers were hurried to safety. Fire hoses froze and the lawn was a crazy quilt of radios, furniture, curtains, lamps, and other office things on Christmas morning in the ice and snow. President Hoover had stood with his guests on the West Terrace, outside the State Dining Room, watching the fire, while inside Mrs. Hoover gathered the frightened children around the Christmas tree and sang carols and distributed presents, diverting their attention from the chaos outside.

Depression times presented a horrible specter beyond the ripply old glass windows of the White House. Inside, the Hoovers trimmed their entertaining to show their awareness of the situation. A servant who had worked at the White House for many years recalled, "Times were terrible, but we [the servants] could pay our rent and we had good meals at the White House."[1] By the end of 1930, the Hoovers were feeding fifty-eight people every day, thirty-two of them servants. For big events, part-time help came and likewise ate at the president's personal expense, an average cost of $2,000 per month, even in those hard times.

Lou Hoover as first lady was very much in charge of the house. The chief usher, Ike Hoover, had come to the White House in 1889 as an electrician, and by 1915 he was in firm control. Although the ghostwriter of his memoirs was later to make snide remarks about the Hoovers, Ike got along with them well, and they always appreciated his abilities. The Hoovers brought in Ava Long as housekeeper, not to dilute Ike Hoover's responsibilities but probably because Mrs. Hoover, like the first ladies immediately before and after her, believed that aspects of the operation of the house needed the female touch. Mrs. Long carried out Mrs. Hoover's wishes concerning food and drink and other details of entertaining, as conveyed by the first lady or one of her social secretaries.

Ike Hoover saw to the direction of the servants on the main floor and the general management and maintenance of the house. He also had ceremonial functions as announcer of important guests. Domestic accounts were kept by Ava Long, a new twist to the usual arrangement that put it all under the chief usher. Mrs. Hoover worked through the housekeeper more than had been the custom at the White House. "Each morning I went through a certain routine," wrote Mrs. Long. "At nine, in my office on the ground floor, I met the chief cook, the butler, the head houseman from each floor, and the carpenter.... If a party were in the offing, I saw also at the morning conference the head flower man, to find out what flowers were available."[2] By this time she had already spoken with the first lady, who knew exactly what she wanted.

With the coming of the Depression, White House functions entered a new era. A tradition since Jefferson's time was the New Year's Day reception at the White House. The event, which was official, had its neighborly side as well in the simple opportunity it provided for people to shake the president's hand. It started at noon, with the arrival of the diplomats; at one P.M. the general public was admitted. It was not unusual for 5,000 callers to pass through the president's receiving line and shake his hand. The reception had become physically arduous by the 1920s. Coolidge, with no plans to return for another term, did not hold it in 1929; but in their enthusiasm, the Hoovers did so in 1930. The president addressed the nation by radio that morning in the West Wing, then went to the house where 6,348 people shook his hand. Two more New Year's receptions were held; then, in 1933 the Hoovers fled to Florida, realizing that they too would not return for another term. The reception was never held again.

In part to escape public life and to flee the hot Washington summers and in part for love of the outdoors and an affection for building that the first lady had, the Hoovers acquired 164 acres in the Blue Ridge foothills of Virginia along the Rapidan River and built a camp. They had no use for the presidential yacht, for they liked the woods. The crew of the yacht *Mayflower* was put into service at Camp Rapidan, which, following the designs of Mrs. Hoover, emerged as a charming frontier "settlement" all in logs and slab shingles, a cluster of buildings in the wildest woods, accessible at first only by horseback. Mrs. Hoover's eye for architecture and design was perhaps sharper than that of any other first lady. Here again she was a modernist; she had remodeled many houses, but built only a few. It had been her taste that was largely responsible for the building on the campus of Stanford University that now serves as the university president's house. When Lou Hoover designed it as her home, she created a stucco reflection of Mexican and Indian California, strong in horizontals, sprawling, and open to the lush plantings that surrounded it. The camp along the Rapidan was charming in that same way, drawing on the imagination of a Daniel Boone past.

The first lady loved the camp. On weekends she departed the White House with a caravan of cars. Just outside the city, she stopped her train, alighted from the limousine, climbed under the wheel of someone's roadster, pressed the gas, and left the procession far behind as she sailed on up the winding, two-lane highway to her retreat. One visitor in 1930 found Camp Rapidan "just as complete as the White House." The president and first lady shared a rustic log structure with deep deck-like porches that seemed to float among the tree limbs.

Here in theory they kept to themselves. However, neither was the type for quiet times very often. They were likely to invite their guests to their private quarters before dinner in the commons cabin. Now and then they ate alone before the fire, tossing pinecones into the flames for the delight of the flares they made. Saturdays and Sundays, when they had the time from work they had brought along, the Hoovers walked the woods paths and crossed the creeks on stepping stones placed there, but looking perfectly natural, at the first lady's behest. She liked to ride horses. Indeed, when she selected the site of Camp Rapidan, she was on horseback, well ahead of a party of military horsemen who trailed her in disbelief along the perilous slopes. Eventually a road was built into the property on the president's amused request, with jokes about saddle sores. Camp Rapidan was donated by President Hoover on his retirement to the National Park Service and is kept in a good state of preservation and used for official meetings.

Home life was always busy for the Hoovers. They converted approximately half the bedrooms on the second floor of the White House into sitting rooms, where they held meetings. It was not unusual for the first lady to have six meetings in a morning. Like the president, she did not linger at these, but moved from room to room, getting right to the point with her callers, solving problems, posing questions. One secretary kept track of details of the Girl Scout business, but Mrs. Hoover was by no means a figurehead. She ran the Girl Scouts.

For the committees of all kinds, including the Scouts, that called at the White House there was necessarily more to the visit than an official agenda. This sort of quasi-business use of the White House was usually enhanced by a hospitable tea. The idea was introduced by Mrs. Hoover, based on the White House tradition of holding dressy teas each week to satisfy minor social obligations (notably returning invitations to visitors, who left calling cards daily at the front door). At her working sessions, Mrs. Hoover must have poured rivers of tea and served mountains of cookies in her four years. She kept these meetings free from the ritualistic structures of the usual social tea parties; they were informal, friendly meetings so that the visitors would not be uncomfortable in the august setting of the White House.

Mrs. Roosevelt would later adopt this tea party pattern, using it as the form for her press conferences, the first ever held by a first lady. There were no press conferences as such under Lou Hoover, although there was constant pressure for some version of them.

Despite a busy schedule, Mrs. Hoover found time to pursue interests in the historic White House. Her fondness for houses, architectural design, and interior decorating made this inevitable. By her time, the White House interiors were considered tired and out of style. In the mid-1920s, a committee had been formed during the Coolidge administration to consider the decorations of the state rooms. Grace Coolidge had admired the new American Wing at the Metropolitan Museum of Art and thought it would be good to have "colonial" furniture in the White House. Most of the committee members had worked on the American Wing as donors. They assumed, wrongly, that they would simply redecorate the White House according to their own ideas. Mrs. Coolidge might have permitted this, but the president stamped his foot and ordered the committee out. Lou Hoover inherited the committee. She recognized its abilities and identified also its arrogance and presumption. But she listened.

The most vocal member of the committee was R. T. Haines Halsey, the well-known collector. Mrs. Harold I. Pratt—Harriet Pratt—was the wisest member, and her husband, a Standard Oil executive, set up a fund that could be spent on furnishing the White House. Other members were Luke Vincent Lockwood, scholar and collector, Mrs. Miles White, Jr., of Baltimore, and two distinguished architects, Charles Pratt and William Adams Delano, both of New York. Halsey had said too much to the press about the tatty White House and annoyed President Coolidge. Coolidge's verbal shotgun blasts, delivered through others, had scattered the committee from the White House, but not cooled its ardor to redecorate and remove all the imitation European furnishings from the rooms in favor of American antiques. Harriet Pratt found social entree to Mrs. Hoover, and soon the committee, although not official, was again making plans for the White House.

Because the state parlors were seedy, their Adamesque, cream colored armchairs repainted so many times that the paint stood in furrows, the curtains moth-eaten, and the whole ensemble a bit too beaux arts for modern tastes, Mrs. Hoover warmed to the idea of a redecoration. She was puzzled by the committee's attitude, believing that as first lady it was her perogative, as it had been with all first ladies, to be involved in the decoration of the house. Yet she wanted what was best for the house, and the president stayed at a distance. He had made his own contribution to history upstairs in originating what he called the Lincoln Study, which he furnished with his personal collection of Lincoln memorabilia. In establishing his study in the room once used by Lincoln for his office, Hoover planted the seed for today's Lincoln Bedroom, which is in the same location.

Mrs. Hoover met with the committee and listened. They proceeded with their plans for the Green Room, but try though she might Lou Hoover could not make much sense out of what they proposed. The committee opted for reproductions of American furnishings, many in their own collections, but not objects ever used in the White House nor even the types of furnishings in style in the early days of the house. Mrs. Hoover went on her way, and the work began in the Green Room. A large cut-glass chandelier was purchased in England. Reproductions of eighteenth- and early nineteenth-century antiques were brought in and placed over a custom-made rug with the presidential seal. New silk damask was acquired for the walls, and matching draperies were hung at the windows.

Mrs. Hoover made some changes at the same time, notably the removal of George Washington's full-length portrait by Gilbert Stuart to the East Room and the pairing of it with an equally large portrait of Martha Washington painted for President Hayes. The Washington portrait is the oldest artifact of continued use in the White House; it is the one Dolley Madison ordered taken to safety in August 1814, just before the British marched on Washington and burned the White House. It still hangs in the East Room where Mrs. Hoover put it. This was not to be her only effort. Uncomfortable with the philosophy—or lack of—that inspired the redecorated Green Room, she sought a more informed approach to the refurbishing of the Executive Mansion.

She asked for historical information about the White House and read Esther Singleton's *The Story of the White House*, which had been published in 1907 in subtle protest against Theodore Roosevelt's 1902 creation of the European look in the first place.

Mrs. Hoover then asked to be shown the historical objects in the house. Was there no inventory or catalog that singled out the authentic pieces from the paint-caked former Green Room chairs? Ike Hoover said no. By 1930 Mrs. Hoover was well along in correcting this. With the assistance of Dare McMullin, an aide, she began the first research program and inventory of the antiques of the White House. She was careful to identify specific antiques that were documented as having been used in the White House in contrast to recent additions from antique shops. McMullin's research was excellent. Days spent in pantries and attics and in the records of the Officer in Charge of Public Buildings (there being as yet no National Archives) revealed a treasure trove. Every object was duly photographed and entered into the catalog, which remains today an indispensable research resource.

Meanwhile, the first lady was decorating upstairs, far from the purview of the committee in the Green Room below. On her arrival she had turned the West Sitting Hall into a tropical remembrance, with tubbed palms, wicker sofas and chairs, and cages of singing birds. This was much more popular with the Hoovers than the sun parlor Mrs. Coolidge had added to the new third floor. Time spent in the White House, however, turned Mrs. Hoover's interest strongly to history and the White House past. Her interest in the past heretofore had been characterized by a certain fascination with antiques and old silks. She had built houses and decorated rooms that evoked the past in a suggestive way; the Stanford house copies nothing, but suggests the adobe past of California; Camp Rapidan evoked the frontier. Mrs. Hoover's view on decorating and building seems to have been this: When one decorates, be subtle and artistic; when one restores, stick to the facts.

When the president created the Lincoln Study, he abandoned the room adjacent to it, which had been the president's study since 1902. We know it today as the Treaty Room, although it had in fact been converted by President Bush into a study again. Mrs. Hoover had furnished it as a bedroom, with odds and ends. It was not used much. The family parlor was the upstairs oval room, over the Blue Room, and here grandchildren and their friends played and the Hoovers sat before cheery fires. Lou Hoover thought the second floor needed a more formal sitting room, so she began making plans for the former study.

Since turning a portion of her attention to White House history, she had begun stopping in her trips to Camp Rapidan by the town of Fredericksburg in Virginia to see the James Monroe Law Office Museum, which had been recently set up to house memorabilia of the fifth president. Among the rich holdings of that select little institution was a group of French furniture pieces—late Louis XVI objects Monroe had purchased in France when he served as minister there under George Washington. Mrs. Hoover was delighted with the sturdy, if fragile-looking chairs, and tables and the handsome fall-front desk on which it is claimed he had written the Monroe Doctrine. The furniture was impeccably documented in history—indeed, it had been central to a scandal when the public learned that President Monroe, by then in retirement, had sold, bought back, and re-sold the furniture to the federal government to raise money for his official tours.

Mrs. Hoover realized that this furniture represented historical fact to which she could respond, not supposition. Dare McMullin pulled out an inventory of the house when Monroe lived there, and she and Mrs. Hoover determined that this very furniture had been used in the upstairs study of the White House. The idea of the new Rose Parlor began to be born in the first lady's mind. This would be a truly historical room and not a fantasy of supposition like the Green Room. In the spring of 1932 Mrs. Hoover, at her own expense, commissioned Morris W. Dove, a Russian-American cabinetmaker in Washington, to reproduce the French furniture exactly as he found it for use in her new upstairs drawing room. President Monroe's descendants were delighted and came forward with additional artifacts and suggestions. They donated a small tea table and a small terracotta vase that had been owned by the Monroes in the White House. At the Smithsonian Dare McMullin found a striking portrait of Mrs. Monroe in black velvet and turban and Mrs. Hoover had it copied for the new room.

Early prints, an 1820s pianoforte, mantel lamps, and one of Monroe's 1818 clocks from the state floor enhanced a setting already coming admirably together. The French style chandelier the committee had discarded from the Green Room provided an elegant complement to the French furniture when at last it was installed. With the walls painted a soft rose, curtains of green satin, and an Oriental rug that left a broad border of polished floor exposed, Lou Hoover completed her drawing room. The first historically "restored" room in the White House—and one of the few ever attempted—the former Rose Parlor soon became known as the Monroe Room.

For all the delights of the entertainments and the renewed interiors, the Hoover White House was often darkened by worry and a sense of futility over the sinking economy. As removed from the situation as we are today, we forget the terrible tensions that the worsening Depression brought and the fear that the governmental system itself might go to ruin. Lou Hoover, who accepted the future's promise and was always one to make way for the new, shared the president's anguish over the nation's hard and emotionally trying circumstances.

When the Bonus Marchers camped out in the nation's capital in 1932 she quietly saw to it that food and blankets were provided. Each day brought desperate appeals from families who sought out the first lady as their last hope. She did not disappoint them, but referred their needs to local agencies and charities. When these public resources proved inadequate she often provided assistance anonymously from her own funds. Eventually these appeals became so numerous that she found it necessary to hire another secretary just to coordinate her informal relief agency. Effective in meeting the needs of others, she was helpless to respond to the critics who painted Hoover as an aloof, do-nothing executive with a heart of cold stone; but she resented them.

Privately she wrote a compelling letter at the White House in the

summer of 1932, just for the record, so that her children and
grandchildren might have her perspective on Herbert Hoover's
efforts in behalf of the "little man." To begin with, she wrote,
"Your father did not want the Presidency . . . for himself, or for the
reputation it might bring him." Rather, he was finally persuaded
by his friends that "if he were President he could give more
opportunity to the least privileged class . . . than he could from any
other point."[3]

Herbert Hoover was defeated in his bid for reelection four
months later, in November 1932. The campaign between Hoover
and Franklin D. Roosevelt was one of the bitterest in American
history, reflecting the times. Roosevelt's inauguration on March 4
was to be the last March inauguration, for Hoover had promoted
and won legislation for the January inaugurations we know today.
The lengthy transition period saw the development of still more
hard feelings when the president-elect refused to endorse Hoover's
plans to combat the nationwide banking crisis, which began in
December 1932. Lou Hoover had hoped to retire in California,
but at the last minute the president decided that he should stay
closer to the pulse of the nation in case he was needed; so they
moved instead to the Waldorf Astoria in New York.

Mrs. Hoover's various personal causes and commitments were
of long standing before she went to the White House. Today a
degree of participation in public service is expected of first ladies,
but she established the idea. Her tenure was markedly different
from those who had gone before. She never varied from the
traditional roles of model wife and hostess demanded of all first
ladies through the long history of the White House; but with that
framework intact, she followed those new paths toward which her
active mind directed her.

She was not to become one of the legendary first ladies because
she simply did not seek self-promotion. Protective of her own
private life, she steadfastly avoided featuring herself in public ways
at the White House. Perhaps, in retrospect, it might be wondered
if the amiable, lively first lady had gone public she might have

counteracted to an extent the bad publicity the president received in being blamed for the Depression.

Every first lady leaves her mark on the White House in some way. Mrs. Hoover's is indelible. Her social changes were practical remodelings and adaptations to make traditional forms more useful. As for the building itself, she drew the first distinction between what one might call "period" interior decoration and the conservation and collection of actual White House historical artifacts. In so doing she started an interest in White House history and restoration that was to be enjoyed and developed by her successors.

Mrs. Hoover and the president entered office in the happiest of periods, with no idea that an era was coming to an end. Their story in the White House has its unhappy side, for no prospects were ever brighter for a president on going there, and very seldom has the turn of events during an administration proved so helplessly disappointing. Some epochs inevitably suffer in hindsight because subsequent events are so highly colored as to block the clear—and accurate—view. Herbert Hoover was blamed for the Great Depression. His one-term tenure in the White House is usually passed over quickly, seen as a time of rising despair leading to a period of solutions under Roosevelt later on. It is thus a sketch, not a finished picture.

The key to a fuller understanding of Hoover's time in the White House may lie less in the president himself than in a closer view of the first lady. Her concept of her purpose in life came from the time when progressive-minded middle and upper-class reformers sought to improve the world. Helping the unfortunate was only one aspect; and although public charity took on greater meaning during the Depression, it was not especially more significant to the original movement before that than, for example, self-improvement, women's rights, artistic development, or progressive farming. Mrs. Hoover's enthusiasm for improvement matches that of any woman in her time, and her interests were quite current. Politically, like the president, she thought in international terms, of the United States as a nation of the world with responsibilities to world peace and the spread of democracy; and she shared Hoover's enormous sense of compassion for those who did not share the freedoms that Americans enjoyed. She had a strong belief in possibility, indeed touched by a certain innocence that gave her convictions vigor. Willing to perform her unpaid White House job faithfully, she yet went her own way and in so doing, she quietly set the pace for first ladies to come.

A world traveler with urbane and sophisticated tastes, Mrs. Hoover was also deeply committed to the encouragement of American artists during the difficult times of the Depression. Her White House musicales drew heavily on American talent.

Chapter 6 ᔐ *Lou Henry Hoover:*
First Lady in the Arts
Elise K. Kirk

When one thinks of artistic first ladies, the first who come to most people's minds are Nancy Reagan who was an actress; Betty Ford, a dancer and student of Martha Graham; or Jacqueline Kennedy, who was knowledgeable in all the arts. But many of our earlier first ladies were performers, arts devotees, and patrons. Frances Folsom Cleveland was an honorary member of the Washington Choral Society and gave her help and support to many struggling young performers and teachers. Before she became first lady, Caroline Harrison, wife of Benjamin Harrison, taught music at the Oxford Female Institute, later part of Miami University in Ohio. Helen Taft was a fine concert pianist who founded the Cincinnati Symphony Orchestra and served as its first president. Woodrow Wilson's first wife, Ellen Axson, was an accomplished painter, and Florence Harding, a former student at the Cincinnati Conservatory of Music, practiced the piano an hour daily while she was first lady. A devoted arts patroness, Grace Coolidge supported the Washington Opera, National Symphony and the New York Philharmonic.

Although she had no formal training in the arts or performing experience, Lou Henry Hoover had broad and long-ranging cultural interests. "She was a liberated woman . . . a genteel lady . . . a connoisseur of beautiful things," noted her niece, Hulda Hoover McLean.[1] An enthusiastic and versatile woman, she also had a lifelong curiosity about the arts and humanities and recognized their value in shaping the human spirit. Music, art, and drama were important elements of education that provided vital dimensions in the personal development of young and old alike. As she said in 1937 while promoting the enjoyment of music at Stanford University: "An engineer, a lawyer, a doctor, a teacher of classics, should be able to get much joy in life with a little more understanding of what music is all about than is just acquired by listening to the radio."[2]

As first lady, Lou Hoover brought a wide variety of performing artists to the White House. These events illustrated not only her dedication to national artistic values, but also her view of the White House as a focal point for the arts. She was the earliest modern first lady to bring black artists to the White House at a time when they were struggling to gain recognition in American theaters. She also responded to hundreds of letters describing the plight of performers, both great and humble, as the Depression intensified. Lou Hoover, moreover, is the only first lady in history whose interest in the arts—especially music—continued long after her White House years. Thus, her vital role in encouraging the performing arts in America, as documented in her papers, provides a unique opportunity for the study of cultural patronage, both political and private, during a critical era in the nation's cultural history.

As a young girl in Waterloo, Iowa, Lou Henry especially loved nature, camping, riding, and the ever-challenging outdoors—but connected to these rugged interests was her joy in the visual and literary arts. Her imaginative sketches of flowers, scenes from California missions and camping life rendered in her early teens show definite talent, and among her more academic literary essays are works of genuine creativity. Her talents in writing appeared early: At age ten she edited her school newspaper, *The Boomerang*; composed a sensitive essay on the American Indian at age twelve and published her first article the following year. Whether skating, collecting specimen spiders, or acting in the class play, young Lou's sense of humor and zest for life are ever present, and her writings throughout high school and college reflect not only an independent young woman but a highly sensitive and perceptive one as well. Just what is an "independent girl?" Lou asked in her essay of 1890. "She delights to find many obstacles in her path, which she overcomes with the skill of a learned engineer, or flanks with tact worthy of a great army strategist. . . . But sooner or later she is sure to meet a spirit equally as independent as her own, and then—there is a clash of arms ending in mortal combat, or they unite their forces and with combined strength go forth to meet the world."[3] And go forth they did. Four years later, Lou Henry met young Herbert Hoover, a fellow geology student at Stanford, and they were married in 1899.

Lou Hoover graduated from Stanford in 1898, with a degree in geology. Her involvement and knowledge in the fields of both science and history are evident especially in the scholarly and literary projects that she undertook after her marriage. By 1907, the Hoovers had traveled around the world five times, and the time they spent in China inspired Lou to publish an article on the Empress Dowager of China. During this time, she also helped her husband write articles and books on mining and collaborated with him on the translation of Agricola's *De Re Metallica*, a sixteenth-century treatise on mining written in Latin, which Mrs. Hoover rediscovered during research at the British Museum in 1906. The drafts of her work suggest that throughout the project she probably did most of the actual translating and writing. During her years as first lady, moreover, Mrs. Hoover applied her versatile talents to the White House when she researched and wrote an ambitious history of the furnishings of the White House. Her concern for historical authenticity led her to furnish one of the rooms (today's Treaty Room) in the period style of James

Monroe—even to the Astor pianoforte made in London between 1799 and 1815, which she borrowed from the Smithsonian.

Although it is uncertain just how frequently Mrs. Hoover attended the theater, the programs among her papers in the Herbert Hoover Library, dating 1911 to 1940, suggest that she attended many performances of plays and musical programs during this period. She also appears to have enjoyed Shakespeare, for there are several programs from Stratford-on-Avon, England, and the Garrick Theatre in New York. Cornelia Otis Skinner, an acquaintance of Mrs. Hoover, played in the Shakespearean comedy, *The Merry Wives of Windsor*, at Washington's National Theatre on November 21, 1927. This and other Skinner programs are part of the collection. While the Hoovers lived in London, the plays of George Bernard Shaw were having a run, and programs from *Man and Superman* and *Pygmalion* are also included. But of all the programs, the musical ones are perhaps the most interesting because they date mainly from the post–White House years when Mrs. Hoover formed the Friends of Music at Stanford. There are concerts of the great Metropolitan Opera baritone Lawrence Tibbett, a personal friend of the Hoovers; the Budapest String Quartet; The Pro Arte Quartet; the San Francisco String Quartet; the Ballet Russe de Monte Carlo; and others—all reflecting the former first lady's fondness for classical music, which was nurtured while she lived in the White House.

Music, however, was never a foreign art to Mrs. Hoover, even before she became first lady. Through music she celebrated many aspects of American life, whether Girl Scouts folk dancing on the White House lawn or diplomats listening to Lawrence Tibbett in the East Room. Arranging concerts for the Pro Arte Quartet of Brussels during its first American tour in 1926 not only reflected Mrs. Hoover's interest in Belgium but also acquainted Americans with one of the finest musical ensembles in the world. She was also interested in personally helping young musicians, and she sponsored concerts in San Francisco's Bay Area for such promising violin virtuosos as Yehudi Menuhin and eighteen-year-old Isaac

Stern, who had made his debut with the San Francisco Symphony at age eleven. Lou Hoover was also a member of the Washington Fine Arts Society, and supported and attended productions of the San Francisco Opera, the Metropolitan Opera, and the struggling young Washington Opera Company for which she was a guarantor while her husband was secretary of commerce from 1921 to 1928.

Mrs. Hoover's patronage of the arts was most visible, however, during her period as first lady and afterward. On January 25, 1932, she sponsored one of the most important concerts ever held in Washington—the performance of the great Polish pianist and statesman, Ignace Jan Paderewski at Constitution Hall. The aging virtuoso drew a crowd of 3,600, raising $11,852.70 in the process for the Unemployment Fund of the American Red Cross. She also sponsored four other concerts that Paderewski gave in various cities to show his appreciation for America's aid to Poland during and after World War I. By the time of his death in 1941 at age eighty-two, Paderewski had known or entertained seven U.S. presidents, but his friendship with the Hoovers was an especially long and close one. Whenever the legendary pianist came to Washington on tour, the Hoovers insisted that he stay in the elegant Rose Bedroom at the White House (today's Queen's Bedroom), and they even placed a Steinway grand piano in his room so that he could practice undisturbed.

When Lou Hoover became first lady, she found a long tradition of White House musical entertainment that dated back to the mansion's earliest days. There had been receptions, luncheons, children's parties, and dances all highlighted by the ubiquitous tones of the United States Marine Band that had been playing at the White House from the days of John Adams in 1801. John Tyler, Abraham Lincoln, Rutherford Hayes and Benjamin Harrison especially enjoyed the wide array of guest artists who entertained them and their guests; but the musicale—the short concert presented in the East Room by invited artists—did not become a firmly established tradition until the early twentieth century under

Theodore Roosevelt. In 1903 the noted American piano firm Steinway & Sons donated the first state concert grand piano to the White House and shortly thereafter the firm began to offer its services in planning White House musicales.

Mrs. Hoover valued the help of Henry Junge, an intellectual, dapper old gentleman with a droll wit and European charm, who worked for Steinway and had been serving as White House arts liaison from the days of Theodore Roosevelt. Knowing all the prominent artists in the music world, Junge recommended appropriate ones to the first lady, scheduled their appearances, suggested their musical selections, and even auditioned their performances. Steinway usually paid their hotels and expenses. Mrs. Hoover held not only thirty-minute concerts after her state dinners but also a series of longer Lenten Musicales, which took place mainly in the afternoons. Typically, two artists appeared on each of these musicales before about 150 to 200 guests. The musicales were familiar to Mrs. Hoover through her predecessor, Grace Coolidge, who had invited Sergei Rachmaninoff, John Charles Thomas, and many other great musicians to perform in the East Room.

The roster of eminent artists who performed for the Hoovers between 1929 and 1933 reads like several seasons at Carnegie Hall. Margaret Matzenauer, Claire Dux, Vladimir Horowitz, Rosa Ponselle, Jascha Heifetz, Albert Spalding, Gregor Piatigorsky, Grace Moore, Carlos Salzedo, Ossip Gabrilowitsch, the Gordon String Quartet, and Paul Shirley—who performed what is most likely the only viola d'amore concert in White House history—were just a few of the luminaries. But although their programs were relatively conservative, Mrs. Hoover's preference for American artists was not. In 1932, at a time in our nation's history when Europeans were capturing the American concert scene, she wrote:

> Even before coming to live at the White House, it used to occur to me as I sat at the musicales after the State dinners, how much more appropriate it would be in this home of the Nation's

President if the music were provided by American artists instead of by the foreign artists who usually come, and whom one hears so constantly at the opera and elsewhere. There are only five or six of these dinners a year, and it seems to me that it might be fairly easy to find enough adequately qualified American artists for the programs on all these occasions. Particularly interesting it might be to find American artists of the coming generation who are just beginning to make their mark in their world, and whose youth and enthusiasm might proudly welcome the opportunity of playing at the White House.[4]

Steinway concurred, and a large number of the artists Henry Junge recommended to the first lady were, indeed, either American-born or naturalized citizens. Several of these young performers such as Lawrence Tibbett from Bakersfield, California; harpsichordist Lewis Richards from St. Johns, Michigan; and harpist Mildred Dilling, from Marion, Indiana; became close friends of the Hoovers.

The brilliant young Metropolitan Opera singer Lawrence Tibbett had been a guest in the Hoover's Palo Alto home and later at their S Street home in Washington. As the election of 1928 approached, Tibbett returned their hospitality: "When you become president, Mr. Hoover, I want to sing at your first White House musicale."[5] Mrs. Hoover made a note of this, and on April 19, 1929, only a few weeks after the inauguration, Tibbett sang four groups of songs and arias in the East Room for a large aggregation of Metropolitan Opera stars and other prominent guests whom the first lady had invited for luncheon. The next day President and Mrs. Hoover heard Tibbett sing in Leoncavallo's *Pagliacci* with the Metropolitan Opera at Poli's Theater in Washington.

Another great singer Mrs. Hoover brought to the White House was Rosa Ponselle, who sang on February 5, 1931, after the dinner for the speaker of the House. The daughter of an Italian baker, Ponselle was born in Meriden, Connecticut, sang professionally at fourteen and became the first American singer without European training to make her Metropolitan Opera debut in a leading role.

105

Critics claimed she colored her tones like an old Italian master painter. And another great singer Geraldine Ferrar believed that the only way one could acquire a voice like Rosa Ponselle's was by a special arrangement with God. The Hoovers and their guests were treated to a rare double bill when Ponselle sang for them on the same program with the renowned violinist Efrem Zimbalist.

Paderewski played his last concert at the White House on November 25, 1930; six weeks later, twenty-seven-year-old Vladimir Horowitz played his first. The young Russian pianist, who already possessed one of the most dazzling techniques of the century, had astounded audiences at his American debut four years earlier. Henry Junge had arranged for Horowitz to perform for President and Mrs. Hoover at a diplomatic dinner on January 8, 1931, but the pianist seemed more concerned about his broken English than his program. "Just say, 'I am delighted,' and nothing more when you pass through the receiving line," Junge advised. Horowitz took the suggestion to heart and greeted the dignitaries with "I am delightful! I am delightful!"[6] No one seemed to mind the error, however. They probably agreed. Horowitz had just played the sparkling, vertiginous *Carmen* paraphrase that later became his signature piece. Indeed, the *Carmen* reappeared forty-eight years later, when Horowitz played for President Jimmy Carter—and the world—in the first White House concert to be publicly telecast.

Visiting heads of state were still rare in America during the Hoover era, and when they did come to the White House they were usually entertained by the Marine Band. Mrs. Hoover, however, was the first to invite a guest artist to entertain a head of state— a tradition that continues today. She invited harpist Mildred Dilling to play for the King of Siam on April 29, 1931, after the state dinner. Dilling was a close friend of Mrs. Hoover and played in the White House three times for her as well as for President and Mrs. Coolidge and for the Roosevelts. By 1939 Dilling had performed 355 times in America, Europe, and Cuba over a five-year period, and in one season alone, she presented eighty-five concerts in the United States. She was also a distinguished harp teacher and counted among her students none other than Harpo Marx.

The large volume of correspondence between Lou Hoover and Mildred Dilling in the Hoover Library reflects a mutual respect and gracious kinship between the two women. "Before you leave the White House," Dilling wrote from New York, "I wish to thank you for the happiness you have given me in letting me play for three of your delightful parties. I am so sorry that you are leaving, and I am sure the White House will miss you as you have made it a friendly place—and with you there I always felt it to be the most beautiful home in our country." Then she added, "You are an inspiration to me—your untiring ability and your thoughtfulness."[7] When Lou Hoover left the White House to reside in California, she arranged to have Dilling present several concerts at Stanford. The harpist's lyric tones were also the last music that Mrs. Hoover heard. She had just returned from a Dilling concert in New York when she suffered a heart attack and died that same evening—January 7, 1944.

The Hampton and the Tuskegee choirs were the first all-black organizations to sing in the White House since the Fisk Jubilee Singers sang for President Chester Arthur in 1882. The Hampton Choir, led by the distinguished American composer R. Nathaniel Dett, was on its way to New York before going abroad "to counteract some of the unfortunate impressions that have been made over there by certain vaudeville and jazz performers during the last few years."[8] The choir sang two numbers on the south lawn of the White House on April 21, 1930. On their return from an engagement at the opening of Radio City Music Hall in early 1933, the Tuskegee Institute Choir performed some new and unusual arrangements in a semi-formal setting at the White House[9] on February 10.

As the 1930s began, unemployment continued to be a grave national concern, and letters to Mrs. Hoover from aspiring artists asking to perform in the White House for the prestige it would bring them increased greatly at this time. People with humble dreams scratched their simple, polite notes on cheap writing paper. A woman whose husband earned $3.50 per week wanted her little girl to dance for the president; a boy asked to bring Rags, his singing dog who said his prayers and told time; members of the Aeolian French Horn Quartet were earning money "to help their parents in hard times." Some of these requests were referred to Henry Junge for auditioning and appraisal; others were turned down graciously.

The last White House concerts of the Hoover years were prophetic. They seemed to foreshadow features that would be continued during the Roosevelt years—in one evening, classical artists would appear with black choirs, Indian, and performers of ethnic music. In other words, there was a tendency to reach out to more varied aspects of the American musical spirit. President and Mrs. Hoover, while differing from the Roosevelts in their musical tastes, undoubtedly felt the need to link the White House programs to the American people more closely as the Depression intensified. Sometimes their "triple bill" resulted in some rather puzzling juxtapositions. The appearance of Mary Garden, a celebrated opera singer, with harpist Mildred Dilling at the diplomatic dinner on February 11, 1933, did not seem too incongruous; but the addition of an American Indian in his colorful native costume did.

Mrs. Hoover invited Chief Yowlache of the Yakima tribe of Washington to sing at the suggestion of Harry Chandler, the owner of the *Los Angeles Times* and a close friend of the president. According to a memo to Lou Hoover from her secretary Ruth Fesler, Chandler advised that a White House concert by Chief Yowlache would be in line with "the president's desire to encourage the Indians to get away from their reservations and take their place in the life of the nation."[10] The concert proved to be one of the most felicitous meldings of music, politics, and protocol ever. For Chief Yowlache amazed the White House guests not only with his beautiful adaptations of Zuni Indian chants but with his lyrical

Italian opera arias. Although, aural documentation of his singing is lost, contemporary reviews indicate that Yowlache possessed a remarkable, truly magnificent voice "more richly endowed than many of his contemporaries who have had an entirely different racial background."[11]

When Lou Henry Hoover left the White House in March 1933, she carried with her the rare and wonderful legacy of music that had enriched her years as first lady. This legacy—together with her friendship with the great arts patron Elizabeth Sprague Coolidge and her sustaining interest in Stanford University—laid the groundwork for the university's excellent Department of Music established less than four years after she died. By arranging a plethora of exceptionally fine concerts, operas, and lectures at the campus, Lou Hoover and Elizabeth Coolidge, both in the final years of their lives, opened a new era in West Coast cultural history.

The story of the early association of the two women and their unique impresarial collaboration is a fascinating one, indeed. Lou Hoover probably first became acquainted with Elizabeth Coolidge when, as the wife of the secretary of commerce, she attended the first concerts held in the Library of Congress's new Coolidge Auditorium. Elizabeth Sprague Coolidge was an extraordinary philanthropist whose generosity and love of music led her to commission many of the greatest works of the twentieth century. She not only underwrote literally hundreds of important premieres and performances both in the United States and abroad but financed the construction of the Coolidge Auditorium, a concert hall that transformed the Library of Congress into an international center for chamber music distinguished to this day.

When Elizabeth Coolidge had lunch one day with the first lady at the White House, Susan Dyer (a former Stanford classmate) recalled, she asked Mrs. Hoover "if there wasn't someplace [on the West Coast] where she could begin to bring her quartets and create an interest in chamber music."[12] Mrs. Hoover helped her get started, first at Mills College, which soon thereafter became an important center for new music, then at Stanford when Ray Lyman Wilbur, a classmate and friend of Herbert Hoover, was president of the university.

Between June 22 and July 27, 1934, the famous Pro Arte Quartet of Brussels—which Mrs. Hoover, in fact, had first brought to Stanford for a concert in 1926—played the entire series of seventeen Beethoven string quartets in six concerts. The series was highly successful, drawing especially large audiences for an area that had little of the East Coast's musical sophistication. "I do hope you know how much this part of the world appreciates what you have done for us with these delightful quartets, and the education it is to so many of our young people as well as pleasure to older ones," Mrs. Hoover wrote to Elizabeth Coolidge on July 14, 1936.[13] Indeed, through her collaboration with Coolidge, Lou Hoover provided Stanford audiences with their first experience in examining and enjoying the world's great string quartet repertoire.

But while Mrs. Coolidge offered to continue her financial support, Lou Hoover felt the community should do its part, too. She decided that an organizing committee should be formed to interest music lovers of the community in raising half the expenses for the continuation of the series. To implement this, she founded the Friends of Music at Stanford in 1937. Her expert managerial skills and dedicated leadership within the society are well documented in the hundreds of letters, memos, and reports among the Lou Henry Hoover Papers. Of special interest are Mrs. Hoover's handwritten notes concerning the society's first constitution, which show that she gave a great deal of time and thought to its rationale, wording and layout.

In 1940, Lou Hoover served as the Friends of Music's first chairperson, underwriting several of the concerts herself. Although her aims were to encourage and support concerts, lectures, and musical instruction, she also hoped that the society would eventually provide funds toward a music library and scholarships for talented students. Her most far-reaching goal, however, can best be summarized in her own words. On August, 14, 1937, she wrote to a potential patron:

> It has always seemed to me a great pity that we did not have a real department of music here, capable of having our graduates leave for the many and diverse fields of life that the University prepares them for with some adequate appreciation of the music that may come their way in the future. . . . I am one of many who have longed for years to have some music courses here for those who are to be busily engaged vocationally or avocationally in other lines. Alas, the University has not had funds to develop sufficiently a department of even this narrow caliber. At present we have a very small department, in fact called a "Division," with only two people on its staff, which does really more than one could expect from such meagre resources.[14]

Before Lou Hoover died on January 7, 1944, the Friends of Music had made possible the engagement of an array of world-renowned faculty and lecturers, such as Herbert Graf, Ernst Krenck, Bela Bartok, Darius Milhaud, Ferenc Molnar, and Nicholas Goldschmidt. Famous artists also performed: William Primrose, Alice Ehlers, Ralph Kirkpatrick, the Roth and the London quartets, and many others. Important premieres were given, such as the first American performance of the entire series of Bach Brandenburg Concertos in their original small ensemble form. Courses in music history, opera and the modern symphony were attended by more than one hundred students, while smaller seminars addressed specific problems in theory and musicology. In short, the Stanford University Department of Music, recognized for its excellence today, was well on its way to its establishment in 1947.

On July 21, 1944, the London String Quartet presented a memorial concert on the campus in memory of Lou Henry Hoover. It played two works of joy, lyricism and power—Schubert's Quintet, Op. 163, and Brahms' Sextet, Op. 18—a fitting tribute to a gracious, dedicated lady. But Mrs. Hoover would no doubt have especially enjoyed the words of a reviewer in the *Daily Palo*

Alto Times, who seemed to capture the true spirit of the Friends of Music: "Through this organization many persons who cannot tootle a flute or saw a fiddle or even carry a tune are becoming active participants in musical expression. When they have paid their subscriptions and become members . . . they are helping give music to the community. This is essentially the American Way, the democratic way. Perhaps then, the Friends of Music should be called the Friends of Democracy as well."[15] Lou Henry Hoover would have heartily agreed.

Chapter 7 ❧ Carrying On:
Lou Henry Hoover
as a Former First Lady

Richard Norton Smith

At the end, the president and first lady went home, to the California house neither had seen for four tumultuous years. For Lou Hoover, the 1932 campaign was a painful reversal of her husband's triumphal progress to the White House. Traveling 12,000 miles in six weeks, she heard cheers from loyal supporters clustered by the thousands around the rear platform of the presidential train. She also heard voices of anger raised in Detroit, New York and other industrial centers. Eggs were tossed and fists raised. The president himself likened the atmosphere on board to that of Warren Harding's funeral train.

After twenty nights spent on swaying railroad cars, Lou was glad to reach California. Yet there was no escaping a sometimes ugly climate fanned by economic hardship and political rhetoric. Sullen crowds stared at the presidential motorcade along San Francisco's Market Street, while Oakland residents jeered openly at the returning chief executive. The mood was very different in Palo Alto, where hundreds of townspeople and students filled the area around Memorial Court.

Inside her house on San Juan Hill the first lady found a

switchboard with forty telephone lines installed in her sewing room. The message they conveyed came with brutal haste. By nine o'clock the following evening, it was clear that 1933 would open a new chapter in Lou's life. Chants of "Sis-boom-bah! President and Mrs. Hoover!" from a crowd illuminated by campus bonfires could neither obscure the magnitude of the president's defeat nor assuage the hurt of popular rejection that November day.

For the moment, the continuing demands of office crowded out thoughts of future employment. Returning to Washington, on the day after Thanksgiving, the first lady took to the radio airwaves with a now familiar appeal. "The winter is upon us," she said. "We cannot be warm, in the house or out, we cannot sit down to a table sufficiently supplied with food, if we do not know that it is possible for every child, woman, and man in the United States also to be sufficiently warmed and fed."[1] A week later, Lou joined other Red Cross volunteers in collecting clothes for impoverished residents of the nation's capital.

A ten day vacation in the Florida Keys afforded the first real chance to ponder the shape of her life after March 4. Her husband confessed his distaste for Palo Alto as a permanent home. It was too isolated from national events, he said, too far from the center of power to satisfy him for more than a few months. Neither could they settle in Washington, where their very presence would invite fresh controversy with the new inhabitants of the White House.

Financial pressures added to the strain of starting over. At the end of January, 1933 Lou outlined for her son Allan the straightened circumstances affecting the entire family. In common with millions of other Americans, the Hoovers had suffered major losses since October, 1929, enough to make the president tell friends that "he really can not consider going into unpaid public service as he had in the past."[2]

At the same time, according to Lou, her husband believed it inappropriate for an ex-president to have even his expenses paid for whatever public service he might render. For the first lady, sacrifice was nothing new. Early in February she wrote to thank

After leaving the White House, Mrs. Hoover resumed her Girl Scout activities full-time but also devoted her energies to groups like the Friends of Music and the Salvation Army. Here she confers with Mrs. Donald McMillan about plans for the Salvation Army's British War Relief clothing drive in 1940.

Allan for accompanying his father on an upcoming fishing trip. "You will be a very bright spot in your daddy's days, and he needs bright spots. He has had a long, dull, deadly grind, and it will be a slow process getting back to ... normal ... like recovering from an illness." Moreover, Lou added, Allan's father liked the boy's sense of humor and point of view. "You are the last touch of cheerful companionship for him." Naturally she would miss him during the time he was away. "But Daddy needs you more than I do."[3]

While the outgoing president grappled with the deteriorating health of the nation's banks and sought, unsuccessfully, to commit Roosevelt to a joint economic program, Lou attended to the social and practical aspects of the interregnum. She welcomed Eleanor Roosevelt for a White House tour and supervised the packing of sixty-nine crates for shipment aboard a naval transport headed for San Francisco. Lou made gifts to the White House staff of glassware, china, pictures and other objects showered upon her and the president during their residence. She presented housemaid Maggie Rogers with a Victrola, and in an example of defiant courage, told Rogers "My husband will come back some day to do great things."[4]

Five thousand people gathered at Washington's Union Station to see the Hoovers off on March 4, 1933. The former president was bound for New York, with Lou accompanying him as far as Philadelphia; there she would join her other son, Herbert, Junior, for the long westward trip across the continent. At Kansas City's Union Station another large crowd, led by Girl Scouts clutching flowers, called for the former first lady. A somewhat different response greeted Lou's husband as he took up temporary residence at New York's Waldorf Towers. Three plainsclothes policemen guarded his suite on the thirty third floor, while outside ugly rumors swirled that Hoover was being watched lest he escape with a hoard of gold. According to one story, the former president was on board Andrew Mellon's yacht, loaded down with gold, and ready to leave New York harbor at any moment.

For both Hoovers, the Wilderness Years had begun. Predictably resentful of such attacks, Lou halted the family's subscription to the *San Francisco Chronicle*, telling her son, "a communist paper could not do better." She turned instead to the *San Jose News*, pronouncing herself astonished "to find how much news it has— good news. And excellent editorials. And what we don't see here—a very good defense of daddy and his administration."[5]

A month later she returned to the subject, expressing shock that any editorial writer could dismiss the Constitution as mere outworn theory.[6] Even as FDR's New Deal programs sailed through Congress, Lou took issue with calls for still more centralization of authority. "Just off hand, I think a balanced system of government, with three wheels interlocking, helping one another in orderly functioning, braking one another when any one gets erratic, is better than any dictatorship," she wrote Allan Hoover. "What do you think about it?" she asked, breathlessly. "Or do you have time to think? I have found a copy of the Constitution and am going to read it!"[7]

Not all the former first lady's time was devoted to constitutional studies. While her husband spent much of his time in a second floor study looking out over San Francisco Bay and a distant Mount Tamalpais, Lou threw herself into campus life and community service. She raised funds for the Stanford Convalescent Home and its programs caring for chronically ill children in their homes. The school's Cap and Gown society held meetings on the Hoover terraces, where magnolias bloomed and buffet suppers featured grilled oysters and miniature enchiladas. Taking an active interest in the university's curriculum, Lou preached the virtues of physical education for all. Working closely with Dr. Helen Pryor, director of the Women's Student Health Service, she helped devise new athletic opportunities for women and professional training for physical education teachers.[8]

At 623 Mirada Drive, the mail continued to pile up, much of it containing requests from souvenir hunters and destitute families familiar to a former first lady. The house was littered with maps—

in desk drawers, in a silver rice bowl, in handbags and coat pockets. But for all the advance planning, Lou was a roving spirit, unable to resist the latent adventure of an uncharted road. She once complimented a friend on a new pair of shoes, even though they were impractical for walking. As for herself, she preferred a pair of white elkskins designed for exploration, not style. A passionate conservationist, Lou took advantage of her newfound freedom to indulge her love of the outdoors. In the summer of 1934 she made an Oregon camping trip along with Bert and Herbert Junior's children, Peggy Ann and Pete. Two years later she toured Mt. Whitney on horseback and the next summer joined Peggy Ann and a friend for an excursion in Yosemite. As late as August, 1941, the 67-year-old former first lady was visiting mining camps in southern Colorado, before hiking, fishing and horseback riding through the rugged terrain of northern New Mexico. At other times Lou enjoyed vacations at Hobe Sound, bicycling along Ocean Road, dismissing bloody wounds caused by a tumble, cooking and eating the sailfish she caught, or tramping through the towering redwoods in girlhood haunts around Monterey.

In the fall of 1933, the Hoovers made a quick trip to Chicago, where the Century of Progress exposition elicited some tart comments. "Parts of it are amusing," she wrote of the fair, "parts amazing; most of it dreary; and all singularly reminiscent of California highway architecture as practiced by filling stations and hot dog stands."[9]

On the way back to Palo Alto, Lou took time out to pronounce a similarly harsh judgment on the New Deal. While most of FDR's emergency measures seemed to be going badly, "all agree that no one should say so publicly yet. . . . That they should go bad of themselves and show their rottenness, not have their backers have the excuse that Republican propaganda killed them."[10] Consistent with this attitude, Lou muted her opposition to Upton Sinclair's 1934 campaign for the governorship of California.

Community Chest drives in Los Angeles and San Francisco took up some of her time and symbolized a lifelong commitment to service. Yet Lou harbored few illusions about human perfectability. In a radio broadcast for the Women's Overseas Service League she harkened back to the Great War: "We who stood facing each other across the broken bodies on those army cots . . . we who would know the sound of singing shell and bursting shrapnel . . . realize now that the war is still on, that it has been going on for thousands of years and will go on for thousands of years to come—the war inside human nature between the helpfulness forces and the selfishness forces."[11]

Asked why she wore so little jewelry, the former first lady replied that as a young woman she could not afford such adornments and now she would rather see the money put to better use— as in helping some other youngster through college. For donation to the Smithsonian's First Ladies Gallery, Lou picked out a gown with no particular historical associations. It was merely a dress she had enjoyed wearing.[12] Her friendship with Elizabeth Sprague Coolidge, who had already endowed a series of chamber music concerts at the Library of Congress, led to the establishment of the Friends of Music at Stanford.

As first lady, she had enjoyed informal parties over starchy receiving lines; best of all, she liked to spontaneously gather a couple hundred Girl Scout leaders for a White House lunch. Two years after leaving the president's house, Lou was re-elected president of the Girl Scouts. The woman who once said she wouldn't know what to do with a daughter gained the next best thing in March, 1937, when Allan married Margaret Coberly of Los Angeles. "Coby," as she was called, became an instant favorite, much admired for an adventurous spirit compatible with her new mother-in-law. A few weeks after their marriage the newlyweds found themselves in a small Iowa town, part of a very personal campaign of historic preservation.

"You know," Lou mused in a rare moment of self-revelation, "young people don't understand loyalty."[13] In the autumn of 1935 loyalty prompted her, working through Allan, to purchase her husband's birthplace at West Branch. For $4,500 she retrieved the white frame cottage, since converted into a summer kitchen for a local family, as the first step toward a park whose growth over the years would mirror the restoration of esteem that came to the man born there more than sixty years before.

It was a typical gesture for the woman Hoover himself called "my good lady who already knows all about a thing or else finds it out."[14] If there was much that the former president guarded from the public, much withheld even from friends, there were no places secret from Lou. When he fell out of popular favor, she drew still more protectively to him. After every speech, he could expect an approving telegram from Lou. When Hoover visited the open range and the scruffy little mining towns that dotted the Rocky Mountains, she was there too, knitting endlessly and laughing easily with the weather beaten miners. (She even taught one pair of Stanford women how to pan for gold in her Palo Alto backyard, complete with a hose for a river and a baked bean lunch for nourishment).

Increasingly restless in his self-imposed California exile, Hoover spent more and more time in the East. He took little part in Alfred M. Landon's 1936 campaign against the New Deal, as his continuing unpopularity made many Republicans distance themselves from their last elected president. Instead of campaign speeches, he pondered a European tour, revisiting the scene of earlier triumphs before returning home to live out his days as an elder statesman. Palo Alto was too provincial to figure in these plans, he said; on that point even Lou seemed to be coming around.

Here Hoover may have been guilty of wishful thinking. For Lou, life on San Juan Hill was a welcome respite from the political wars. She took naturally to the casual pursuits of a college town. On sunny days the former first lady carried a shopping bag along University Avenue, pausing to exchange stories with old friends and plan picnics in the hilly, moorlike region that she called Scotland. Lou's sons and grandchildren lived nearby. The countryside of her girlhood beckoned; so did the quail on her lawn and the oriole in a pepper tree. "You are missing most heavenly cherry blossoms, wisteria, lilacs and bulbs from your study window,"[15] she wired her traveling husband on April 21, 1937.

Actually she had little time in which to admire nature's bounty. Beginning in 1937 Lou took an active role in the Salvation Army, planning bazaars and organizing fundraising dinners. She was less enthused about a proposed radio broadcast featuring America's four other surviving First Ladies discussing the peacemaking efforts of their husbands. She took the request lightly "because I never yet have found any of these many attempts to get them all to do anything to succeed. It seems always to be done either by rather crude advertisers . . . or naive and erratic welfare organizations."[16]

She was similarly reluctant to join a committee to promote better housing conditions, a cause near her husband's heart during his days as secretary of commerce and president. She had already said no to Ray Lyman Wilbur when that good friend asked her to be a part of a campaign against "social diseases." Her invariable response to such invitations was "that my time is so occupied that I can not assume any further obligations, and that it is my custom not to take positions on honoring or sponsoring committees where I may not keep pace with activities of the organization."[17]

Good women through their indifference pave the way for bad politicians—so Lou had always claimed. As the 1930s neared their end and the nation's economy remained depressed, the former first lady edged cautiously into the arena of partisan activity. Practical as ever, she confessed to her friend Sue Dyer that opposition to the New Deal was more important than "rigidly . . . Republican"[18] sentiments. Accordingly, in 1938 she became a dues paying member of Pro America, an organization to which the Republican National Committee gave its belated blessing in 1939. Lou felt no more enthusiasm for Wendell Willkie's presidential candidacy the next year than her husband had mustered for Landon's doomed effort in 1936.

Mrs. Hoover remained stateside when the former president

traveled through Europe in 1938. She was at a Girl Scouts regional office in Salt Lake City in August of that year, when Bert telegrammed his intentions to send a "prize rainbow . . . enough to feed your whole camp for a week"[19] caught on his birthday in the Canadian Rockies. Six months later the Hoovers were again separated, when a telegram arrived in Palo Alto bearing the names of Bert, Herbert Junior and his wife Peggy, plus Allan and Coby.

"We are having a party to celebrate the fortieth anniversary," it read. "Its deficiency is that you are not here. But we have in it all the affection that you could wish and another forty years is indicated. We are sending an appropriate mark of the occasion in a few days."[20]

By now the former president was a more or less permanent resident of New York, where he was occupied with his Committee on Food for the Small Democracies. Questioned by reporters as to her own contributions, Lou inevitably fell back on her most cherished youth group. The Girl Scouts could set an example for all Americans, she asserted. Girls who had fled to the United States to escape political persecution abroad were warmly welcomed, and gifts of American money and clothing were shared with scouting groups in Germany, Italy and the Soviet Union—until foreign governments discontinued Girl Scout programs.

In May, 1940, Lou joined women's committees extending assistance to occupied Belgium and France. Soon after she accepted the chairmanship of a Salvation Army effort enlisting schoolchildren in twelve western states to fill a ship with winter clothing for European children. Before the year was over, Lou could report to her fellow volunteer Mary Pickford that 1,000,000 pounds of clothing was on its way to Great Britain, with contributions still coming in. "I do think that is a remarkable achievement in such short time as they had, do you not?"[21]

Lou would clothe beleaguered Britain, but she could not close her eyes to military negotiations involving the swap of fifty U.S. destroyers for British bases in the New World. In her indignation she even accepted an invitation from Nebraska Republicans to go to Lincoln at the end of October, 1940, where her husband was to deliver a major address critical of Roosevelt's foreign policy.

A few days later FDR was re-elected to a third term. Hoover decided to sell his house on Washington's S Street. That same month Lou received yet another message from her partner in New York. "I have secured a very much more comfortable apartment in the Waldorf Towers for the winter. I think it would be a good thing for you to come along. Take a look at the arrangements and camp here."[22]

"You know," Lou once remarked. "I've never yet seen a room I didn't want to do something *to*."[23] Fresh flowers and favorite pictures testified to her knack for creating a home out of a hotel room. Henceforth home was the elegant Waldorf Astoria, whose inhabitants included the Duke and Duchess of Windsor, the future Shah of Iran, and Cole Porter. Lou's new abode was a self-contained community, protected by a small army of security guards, backed by interpreters conversant in dozens of languages, 155 telephone operators and no fewer than 200 cooks. At Christmas, Lou threw a party for hotel employees—it was her pleasure, she explained to one waiter, to serve him for a change.

With typical aplomb, the outdoorswoman adapted to city life. Friends calling for dinner one evening were surprised not to see her at the table. "She's there," the former president told them with a wave of his hand, "under the table . . . a light went out, and she knows all about these things so I let her fix them."[24]

Without missing a beat, Lou climbed to her feet and extended her hand. "How do you do?"[25] she said.

Beneath her placid exterior, the former first lady harbored fierce resentments. She never forgave Japan for overrunning her beloved China. Yet her abhorrence of war enforced silence during a time of mounting international tension. So it came as doubly shocking to her niece, Hulda, late in November, 1941, when Lou, visibly upset, announced, "We're going to have war with Japan." The younger woman asked for an explanation. "Cordell Hull has written a note to the Emperor that means war,"[26] Lou replied. By then her husband had reached the end of his own tantalizing negotiations through a New York lawyer with connections to the Japanese embassy in Washington.

Kept out of the war effort himself, Hoover tried to influence postwar arrangements with his pen. Lou monitored the sales of his 1942 volume, *Problems of Lasting Peace*, but by then her own fabled energy was beginning to flag. For nearly half a century she had remained at Bert's side, uprooting herself and her family whenever a new mine or continent beckoned. "I am a lucky woman to have had my life's trail alongside the paths of three such men and boys,"[27] she wrote in the autumn of 1943.

A year earlier she had composed a still more revealing letter to a putative biographer. "I am simply appalled by the adjectives . . . I can think of nothing but a blue pencil," she admonished her correspondent. "Nor can I but smile at the 'no taste for a career'— for, depending exactly upon what one's definition of 'career' may be, I have not said that!" A wistful note crept into her words. "All kinds of projects I should like to have put through. A number of professions or callings I should like to have followed, and was prepared to begin. But always duties, interests, activities or the moment, pushed farther back the moment for taking up any long-to-be continued cause or profession."[28]

Gentle sarcasm tinged Lou's reaction to another claim. "I love to settle back," she wrote impishly, "with a feeling of being 'gentle, coupled with a passive nature.'"[29]

At Christmas, 1943 Lou mailed money to a former White House maid, with instructions to buy Christmas presents for her children.[30] On January 5, she went to a concert by Mildred Dilling, a harpist who had once graced the East Room. Leaving the performance, she told her companion that the air felt good; why not walk home. A short while later she changed her mind, and hailed a taxi. Back at the Waldorf she went to her room. Later, when Bert stopped to tell her that he was leaving for an engagement, he found her sprawled on the floor. A house doctor was sent for, but within a few minutes Bert reappeared in the living room to announce that she was gone.[31]

Three days later, fifteen hundred mourners gathered in St. Bartholomew's Episcopal Church, just across the street from the Waldorf. The chairman of the American Friends Service Committee read passages from First Corinthians, Revelation, and the Gospel of Saint John. There was no eulogy. Two hundred Girl Scouts were there, along with Joseph P. Kennedy, Eddie Rickenbacker, Roy Howard, and Mrs. Wendell Willkie. Later that day, a train headed west, bound for Palo Alto, where Lou would rest for twenty years, until her husband's death in October, 1964, when her remains were reinterred next to his on a gentle hillside overlooking the two-room cottage where he was born.

When the grieving widower went through Lou's desk at the Waldorf, he found it filled with uncashed checks, repayments of assistance lent to strangers as well as friends, students seeking college tuition, mothers worried about infants, old people shunted aside to fend for themselves. It was a final surprise from a woman who fit no stereotypes or pigeonhole. Yet it could not surprise those who knew the real Lou.

Quiet moments at Rapidan Camp in the nearby Blue Ridge mountains provided a welcome escape from the demands of the Presidency. Mrs. Hoover's papers reveal, however, that the Camp was also the scene for meetings with Girl Scout leaders and world figures such as British Prime Minister Ramsay MacDonald. The Girl Scouts' innovative relief plan, which is discussed in chapter 5, was worked out in a 1931 meeting at Camp Rapidan.

Chapter 8 ❧ The Documentary Legacy of Lou Henry Hoover

Dale C. Mayer

The American people have had a deep and abiding interest in the wives of their presidents even though the historical record concerning them is relatively sparse. Most Americans are familiar with Martha Washington, Mary Todd Lincoln, Eleanor Roosevelt, and the more recent first ladies, but their knowledge of them is very superficial. Efforts to learn more about earlier first ladies have been frustrated because their personal papers have not survived—a problem that is reflected in the dispersal and relative scarcity of presidential papers prior to those of William Howard Taft. The period of more extensive documentation of first ladies' activities begins with the 27 linear feet (less than 20,000 items) of personal papers preserved by Edith Galt Wilson. The earliest collection to provide a full-length portrait of a first lady, however, is that of Lou Henry Hoover.

Unlike the papers of many other notable Americans, Mrs. Hoover's papers (141 linear feet and over 220,000 items) provide coverage of all of the important stages of her life—from her formative adolescent years in California through the trials and tribulations of the White House years to her return to California in 1933. Opened to scholars and the public alike in the spring of

1985, the papers offer many opportunities to assess her place in women's history and to provide innumerable insights into the personality, attitudes, and fascinating life of one of the most intriguing women ever to have presided as first lady.

The Personal Correspondence series of Mrs. Hoover's papers is divided into four chronological segments, each period having its own distinctive physical characteristics and subject matter. For example, correspondence from 1914 to 1933 consists mainly of incoming letters and replies by secretaries. During this period Mrs. Hoover relied on a succession of aides and secretaries to answer letters from the public and to keep track of her social calendar. Due to the volume of her mail, frequent absences, and a very crowded schedule, even old friends often found themselves communicating through intermediaries to conduct *business* matters. Personal matters involving friends received Mrs. Hoover's attention, but replies often were delayed by her frequent travels.

Correspondence from the post–White House years suffers less from the intrusion of secretaries and has a more personal flavor. White House social demands were replaced with more satisfying activities on behalf of the Friends of Music, the Salvation Army, Stanford and Palo Alto groups, and her beloved Girl Scouts. A less crowded calendar also seems to have allowed her to take a greater interest in her correspondence with friends and fellow Girl Scouts. Biographers will find important insights into her personality and character in numerous letters from her friends that continually pay tribute to her kindness, wisdom, generosity, and buoyant spirit. Her own letters reveal all of these traits plus a total disinterest in social climbing and pretense, a dedication to public service, a lively sense of humor, and a zest for living.

Some of the earliest and most numerous items in the collection are letters to and from various family members and relatives. Although this correspondence stretches over her entire lifetime, these early letters are especially interesting and significant. Until these letters became available in 1985, information concerning the years spent at Stanford, the early years of their marriage and Mr.

Hoover's mining career had been very limited. Fortunately, Mrs. Hoover's letters to her parents have survived and one is now able to piece together more of the details from the period between 1892 and 1921.

Beginning in 1892 when she was a student at San Jose State Normal School, these letters often seem oddly familiar. Reflecting concerns that seem typical of middle-class parents of every age, Charles Henry inquires about college expenses and always closes by sending his love. Lou's mother offers advice on manners, grooming, and the recycling of dresses; expects reports on where her daughter went, what she wore, how she looked, and who she saw; and wonders, with bewildered parents of all eras, why letters home are not more numerous. The letters also indicate that the Henrys understood their daughter's need to assert her independence and find a vocation that would be both challenging and fulfilling.

Although highly interesting, Mrs. Hoover's pre-1914 correspondence does, unfortunately, have its limitations. There is relatively little, for example, about the Hoovers' travels in Russia, France, and the British Isles or about the literary-minded set in which they occasionally found themselves. The Hoovers were voracious readers who devoured fiction and nonfiction with equal relish. Their letters from China contain reminders to sister Jean to maintain the steady flow of books and magazines and include descriptions of the kinds of literature that interested them. Hoover acquaintances during the so-called London years (1905-1917) include Mary Austin, John Maynard Keynes, Joseph Conrad, and H. G. Wells. They also probably knew Rudyard Kipling and Arthur Conan Doyle.

Another limitation stems from the lack of information about the inner circle of the Hoover family. Domestic details, particularly during the London years, are few and far between. There are no letters—not even to her mother—announcing pregnancies; only a single letter the day before the birth of Herbert, Jr., concerning the completion of a dress for the baby. The few details in the collection concerning the birth of the first child are supplied by Lou's diary and sister Jean, who was staying with the Hoovers in London.

In later years, the amount of information increases with reports from nurses and teachers concerning the boys' activities. During the 1920s there are also some reports on Allan Hoover's progress in school and daily activities in letters from the tutor-companions that Mrs. Hoover recruited from the ranks of Stanford graduate students. These letters provide some insight into Lou's concern about her sons and offer a few glimpses into the Hoovers' values and attitudes on the subject of child rearing.

Despite frequent absences on Girl Scout or Commerce Department business, the Hoovers were a close-knit family who made the most of their moments together. During the Commerce years, Mr. Hoover found the time to take his sons to baseball games, on spur-of-the-moment fishing trips, and even though he is not known to have played the game, on at least one golf outing. On another occasion, one of Mrs. Hoover's secretaries reported to her that the secretary of commerce spent several hours on successive evenings helping his sons select recordings to order for the family's new phonograph.

Additional insights into family activities and interaction may also be forthcoming in addition to Allan Hoover's papers that covers both the early years as well as the 1920s and 1930s. These letters have just been opened and not much is known about their contents at this time. They are expected, however, to provide information that was previously not available in other sources.

The content of the Personal Correspondence series runs the gamut from valuable insights to trivia. However, the persistent researcher will find many nuggets and one never knows what the turn of a page will produce. Two letters written in 1914 provide insights into Lou's beliefs and the serious, thoughtful side of her personality. In November 1914, before setting out across waters infested by U-boats to rejoin her husband in London, she asked Jackson Reynolds, a Stanford classmate, to assume responsibility for her sons if something should happen to her and her husband during their wartime travels. This letter provides important insights into her beliefs and values and reveals a loving and wise mother's aspirations for her sons.

She was convinced that Reynolds possessed the "right balance to make good men out of my boys, physically, intellectually, and in the yet higher things" and that he would not allow them "to get a money measure for all the affairs of life." In its place she hoped that "the ambition to do, to accomplish, irrespective of its measure in money and fame . . . should be inculcated."[1]

Among the "yet higher things" was a belief in a divine providence that formed the core of her religious beliefs. She detailed these beliefs in an unusually long and especially poignant letter that she gave to Reynolds for possible delivery to her sons in the event of her death. The letters were later returned to her and now reside with the rest of her papers at the Hoover Library.

Another very interesting letter was written in June 1932 to her children and grandchildren. In a rare and candid display of indignation, she analyzed the lack of fairness in the current campaign rhetoric, which pictured her husband as aloof and having no feeling for the plight of the "little man in the street."[2] In addition to providing an extended defense of her husband, the letter also contains some very interesting comments on his previous record as an enlightened employer, his decision to run for the presidency in 1928, and the immense personal and financial sacrifices he had made while directing relief activities during and after World War I. Significantly, the letter provides—for perhaps the first time—direct testimony to the emotional toll exacted by Hoover's frequent confrontations with tragedy while on inspection trips in areas immediately behind the lines during the war.

Finally, there is a very brief exchange of cables in 1915 between Hoover and Stanford President David Starr Jordan. Stanford grads in Manila had asked Jordan to sound out Hoover on the approaching presidential primaries. "Would Hoover accept Republican nomination for Presidency?" Jordan cabled. Mrs. Hoover replied for her husband, "I think that you had reached the age of discretion enough to have sent in an emphatic denial . . . the only difference in your answer and Bert's would doubtless have been that his would have been much more emphatically expressed."[3]

Other portions of Mrs. Hoover's papers—from a wide-ranging Subject File series to her files on the White House years and her involvement with the Girl Scouts—contain equally interesting information. The globe-trotting years from 1899 to 1912 are sparsely documented in diaries and family correspondence— except for one cataclysmic event, the Boxer Rebellion. It appears that the Hoovers had decided to chronicle their stay in China in a series of magazine articles written from the perspective of traveling Westerners. Once the Boxer uprising had taken place, they obviously decided to enlarge their project to book-length proportions. Many quickly produced accounts that appeared soon after the uprising had been crushed contained inaccuracies; the Hoovers hoped to produce an accurate account based on their own experiences. However, business pressures and other priorities intervened and the nearly completed book was never published.

But, the final draft and diaries of other participants may be found in the Subject File series of Lou's papers. Letters to her parents, written just before the siege of Tientsin, discussing the challenges of establishing their new home in a new cultural setting and the difficulties of adjusting to Chinese customs, are in the Personal Correspondence series. In addition to presenting an interesting picture of their daily life, Lou's papers provide some interesting commentary on conditions in China at the time and the background of that explosive period. In 1900 China was poised, at the end of a very corrupt and self-indulgent dynasty, on the brink of the democratic reforms that were to shape its history for the next fifty years.

Reflecting the Hoovers' typical modesty, the papers contain very few details of the Hoovers' participation in the Boxer Rebellion. There are some references in letters after the fact and a few fleeting references are buried in the Boxer book drafts. There we learn, for example, that Mr. Hoover served as a guide for one combat patrol and was shot at and that Lou had the tires of her bicycle riddled by gunfire while on an errand of mercy. The record of the Hoovers' participation in World War I is more complete than the account of their activities during the Boxer Rebellion.

Documentation of the efforts of the American Committee in London to assist American tourists at the beginning of the war is a bit sparse. The files concerning the efforts of the Society of American Women in London are not only more voluminous but much more informative. Files that refer to Belgian relief and the sale of Belgian lace are modest both in quantity and information. The same may be said of documents that reveal Mrs. Hoover's interest in the activities of the Food Administration, the Food Administration Women's Club, and the Canteen Escort Service of the Red Cross.

Additional documentation of the Hoovers' activities during the war and immediate postwar period (1914–1921) can be found in the Personal Correspondence series. This correspondence continues through the period (1921–1928) when Mr. Hoover served as secretary of commerce. The largest single file for the Commerce Department period concerns social engagements; but there are several scattered files in the Subject File series, largely of a personal nature, dating from the 1920s. Perhaps the most informative of these, which contains correspondence with and about a variety of servants and secretaries, may be found in the Subject File under the heading Servants and Aides.

Perhaps the most significant of all of Mrs. Hoover's World War I activities were the Girl Scouts. Having grown up, with her father's encouragement, as a tomboy, Lou later would fondly recall that her interest in the outdoors, which eventually led to her commitment to the Girl Scout movement, began "when my father took me hunting, fishing and hiking in the mountains."[4] A personal invitation in 1917 from Juliette Low to assume responsibility for a troop of Washington Girl Scouts soon led to an invitation to serve on the National Board of Directors. As she became more familiar with the organization she came to the conclusion that "here is what I always wanted other girls to have."[5]

Mrs. Hoover's contributions to the growth of the Girl Scout movement included multiple terms as president, honorary president, and national board member extending without a break from 1917 until her death in 1944. Her papers provide details revealing her enormous success as a fund-raiser and the impact of her sage counsel and harmonizing influence in the movement. An important supplement to her scouting files can be found (in the Subject File series) in copies of statements and articles (1918–1942) in which she espouses the Girl Scout philosophy.

Without a doubt the most extensively documented years of Lou's life are the White House years. One important feature of her papers is their ability to capture so much of the flavor and substance of those years. Descriptions of the ceremonial functions, the sumptuous dinners and receptions, the constant stream of requests from constituents, her informal relief network during the depression, and weekend trips to Camp Rapidan to escape Washington's legendary heat are readily available in her White House files. In sharp contrast to the papers of her predecessors, the papers of Lou Henry Hoover provide a comprehensive picture of the daily comings and goings of a busy first lady.

Correspondence, clippings, and photographs concerning the school the Hoovers established near Camp Rapidan may be found in the Rapidan Camp files in the Subject File series. One very touching document contains the observations of a team of educators and child psychologists who interviewed the children and adults in that remote hollow before the school opened.

Students of the White House itself will welcome Lou's personal research into the history of the executive mansion and the families that had lived there. The results of her research have survived in a carefully documented, though unpublished, manuscript on the history and furnishings of the White House complete with photographs of Hoover White House interiors.

As mentioned earlier, the post-presidential years are also well documented in the Personal Correspondence and Subject File series and in the files of the Professional and Organizational Activities series. These materials reflect Lou's activities on behalf not only of the Girl Scouts but dozens of other organizations, notably the Friends of Music, the American Red Cross, the Salvation Army, and numerous Palo Alto groups.

Her place in women's history remains to be fully assessed, however. Born at the height of the Victorian era, she seems to have possessed a more modern outlook on life than many of her contemporaries. Comparisons with present feminists suggest that her views on the possibility of combining a family and a career were transitional and might be worthy of further investigation and discussion. She certainly would have been an unforgettable person to have known and now, through the vehicle of her personal papers, it is possible for all of us to know and understand her better.

Viewed collectively, the Lou Henry Hoover Papers are truly a remarkable historical and cultural resource. Their scope and size combine to provide a fairly complete, self-contained portrait of a fascinating woman, the times in which she lived, and the events in which she participated—and helped to record. Thus, many of the fascinating aspects of the collection are directly attributable to her zestful approach to life. Always ready to experience something new, Lou Henry Hoover reached out to embrace all of life's worthwhile possibilities. The consequences of that approach to life are very much in evidence throughout her papers.

Notes ❧

The following abbreviations have been used to designate segments of the Lou Henry Hoover Papers (LHHP) in the custody of the Hoover Presidential Library, West Branch, Iowa (HHPL):

PC	Personal Correspondence series
SF	Subject File series
WHGF	White House General File series
POA	Professional and Organizational Activities series
AAS	Articles, Addresses and Statements file
GSAC	Girl Scouts Administrative Correspondence file

Introduction: A Quick Review of a Busy Life

1. Florence Henry to Mrs. Mason, March 12, 1899, Hoover, Lou Henry: Marriage Ceremony and Honeymoon, SF.
2. Dudley Harmon, "Dining with the Hoovers," *Ladies Home Journal* (March 1918).
3. *Toledo* (Ohio) *Times*, February 13, 1932, AAS, SF.
4. *Duluth* (Minnesota) *News Tribune*, May 27, 1936, AAS.

Chapter 1: Lou Henry Hoover: Emergence of a Leader, 1874–1916

1. Lou Henry Hoover (hereafter LHH) to Jackson Reynolds, November 24, 1914, Reynolds, Jackson, PC.
2. LHH to Herman L. Perry, May 7, 1937, PC.
3. LHH to Henry Heinkel, February 10, 1938, Family History and Genealogy, SF.

4. LHH Composition Notebook, ninth grade, Curator's Collection, LLHP.
5. Los Angeles Normal School Notebook, 1891, SF.
6. *Idem.*
7. Diary entry, October 29, 1891, SF.
8. Calie Cook's Alumni History of Whittier School, 1894, Family History, SF.
9. Secretary of Mines to LHH, December 15, 1905, London, England, 1902-1906, 39 Hyde Park Gate, S.W. "Flat," Hoover Homes Collection, HHPL.
10. John Casper Branner to LHH, November 20, 1905, Branner, John and Susan, PC.
11. LHH to Jackson Reynolds, November 24, 1914, Reynolds, Jackson, PC.
12. LHH to Charles Henry, December 10, 1901, PC.
13. *Idem.*
14. Albert Whitaker to LHH, July 23, 1898, Wa-Wh Misc., PC.
15. LHH to Wayne Whipple, June 26, 1929, Family History: Wedding, SF.
16. Herbert Hoover, *The Memoirs of Herbert Hoover: Years of Adventure* (New York: Macmillan, 1951), p. 23.
17. Lou Henry Hoover to Evelyn Wight Allan, undated (ca. August 8, 1900), Evelyn Wight Allan Papers, HHPL.
18. Handwritten draft of experiences in Boxer Rebellion: Drafts (Early): History of Inside the Circle, SF; Herbert Hoover, *The Memoirs of Herbert Hoover: Years of Adventure* (New York, Macmillan, 1951), p. 50.
19. Frederick Palmer, "Mrs. Hoover Knows," *Ladies' Home Journal*, 46 (March 1929): 6, 242.
20. John H. Means to John C. Branner, July 9, 1900, Branner papers, Box 13, Stanford University Archives.
21. LHH to Evelyn Wight Allan undated (August 1, 1900), Evelyn Wight Allan Papers, HHPL.
22. Arline Golkin, "The China Years," paper presented March 9, 1991, Hoover VIII Symposium, George Fox College, Newberg, Oregon.
23. *New York Times*, 1928, Duplicate Printed Material, Agricola Collection, HHPL.
24. Hazel Lyman Nickel, "A Chained Book—Now Free to All," *The Canadian Mining and Metallurgical Bulletin* (June 1949): 305, Duplicate Printed Material, Agricola Collection, HHPL.

25. Nickel, "A Chained Book," p. 305.
26. Letterhead of the Friends of the Poor, POA.
27. A. N. Collin to LHH, October 17, 1912, Friends of the Poor, POA.
28. Constitution, Article II, American Women in London, POA.
29. Mrs. Webster Glynes to LHH, April 2, 1908, American Women in London, POA.
30. Lucy Allen Selwyn to LHH, June 29, 1913, American Women in London, POA.
31. Jennie T. Comings to LHH, November 9, 1910, American Women in London, POA.
32. Jennie T. Comings to LHH, January 9, 1914, American Women in London, POA.
33. *Idem.*
34. Western Union Cable, May 24, 1914, American Women in London, POA.
35. Herbert Hoover to Walter Hines Page, September 23, 1914, American Citizens' Committee—London, Subject File—Herbert Hoover Pre-Commerce Papers, HHPL.
36. LHH to Mrs. John Lewis Griffiths, January 29, 1915, p. 5, American Women's War Relief Fund, SF.
37. The Duchess of Marlborough was the American-born Consuelo Vanderbilt.
38. LHH to the Duchess of Marlborough, January 23, 1915, American Women's War Relief Fund, SF.
39. LHH to Mrs. John Lewis Griffiths, January 29, 1915, pp. 4–5, American Women's War Relief Fund, SF.
40. Report of the President of the Society of American Women in London for the Year 1915, American Benevolent Committee, SF.
41. *Idem.*
42. *Idem.*
43. *Idem.*
44. *Idem.*
45. *Idem.*
46. *Idem.*
47. *Idem.*
48. LHH to Evelyn Wight Allen, June 16, 1898, PC.

Chapter 2: "Don't Forget Joy!": Lou Henry Hoover and the Girl Scouts

1. Comments at regional Girl Scout conference in Davenport, Iowa, April 28, 1937, AAS, SF.

2. Hoover, Lou Henry: Death and Funeral—Memorials and Tributes: Girl Scouts, a Tribute from, pp. 8–9, SF.
3. LHH to Mrs. Paul Rittenhouse, July 1, 1936, Lou Henry Hoover Correspondence, National Historic Preservation Center, Girl Scouts of the USA Headquarters, New York, New York.
4. Address at DAR Meeting in Washington, D.C., April 22, 1927, AAS, SF.
5. *Idem.*
6. Untitled article, *American Girl*, volume 5, number 7, April, 1922, p. 4.
7. LHH to Katerine Everts, March 26, 1925, Girl Scouts: Administrative Correspondence, GSAC, POA.
8. Address at Girl Scout annual convention, Boston, October 26, 1934, AAS, SF.
9. Undated clipping fragment, ca. 1923, *Portland Tribune*, AAS, SF.
10. LHH to Genevieve Brady, April 14, 1930, GSAC, Brady, G., POA.
11. LHH to Esther S. Dickerson, October 22, 1923, GSAC, POA.
12. Opening address at Girl Scout annual convention, San Francisco, October 2, 1935, AAS, SF.
13. LHH, President's report at Girl Scout annual convention, Washington, D.C., April 25, 1923, AAS, SF.
14. Comments at Girl Scout national convention in Savannah, January 25, 1922, AAS, SF.
15. Oral history interview with Gertrude L. Bowman, pp. 16–17, Herbert Hoover Oral History Program (hereafter HHOP).

Chapter 3: Lou Henry Hoover and Women's Sports

1. Opening remarks by LHH at NAAF conference, Washington, D.C., April 6, 1923, AAS, SF.
2. Foreword, *Play Day: The Spirit of Sport* (Washington, D.C.: American Child Health Association, 1929), p. 10.
3. *New York Herald*, March 25, 1923.
4. Report by Elwood Brown to NAAF board of governors, December 3, 1923.
5. Unsigned letter to Thomas Storey (probably from Susan B. Bristol), April 16, 1923, NAAF: Annual Meeting—Storey, Thomas, POA.
6. Quoted in *Idem.*
7. Opening address at Second Annual Meeting of the NAAF, December 31, 1923, NAAF Men's Division: Annual Meeting, 1923, POA.
8. Opening remarks by LHH at NAAF conference, Washington, D.C.,

April 6, 1923 in NAAF Women's Division: Annual Meetings: 1923—Opening Address by LHH, POA.

9. Resolutions adopted by the Conference on Athletics and Physical Recreation for Women and Girls, Washington, D.C., April 6–7, 1923, NAAF Women's Division: Annual Meeting, 1923—Resolutions, POA.

10. Lillian Schoedler, Report of Progress to Women's Division of the NAAF, June 1924.

11. Remarks by LHH.

12. Platform of the NAAF adopted at the seventh annual meeting in Detroit on April 1, 1931, NAAF Women's Division: Policy and Platform, POA.

13. *Pittsburgh Sun*, May 4, 1923.

14. LHH speech at a Girl Scout mass meeting in Milwaukee as reported in the *Milwaukee Sentinel*, May 19, 1927, AAS, SF; LHH to Zelma Boeshur, May 26, 1921, Hoover, Lou Henry: Professions for Women—Views On, SF.

15. LHH membership solicitation letter, 1923, NAAF: Women's Division.

16. LHH in *Play Day: The Spirit of Sport* (Women's Division, National Amateur Athletic Federation, 1929), p. 10.

17. *Ibid.*, p. 12.

Chapter 4: A Neglected First Lady: A Reappraisal of Lou Henry Hoover

The author extends special thanks to Nancy Beck whose thorough research in the papers of Mrs. Hoover made this essay possible.

1. The historical literature on Lou Henry Hoover is very limited. The only biography, long out of print, is Helen Pryor, *Lou Henry Hoover: Gallant First Lady* (New York: Dodd, Mead and Co., 1969). Dale C. Mayer, "An Uncommon Woman: The Quiet Leadership Style of Lou Henry Hoover," *Presidential Studies Quarterly* 20 (Fall 1990): 685-698, is based on extensive work in Mrs. Hoover's papers.

2. Myra G. Gutin, *The President's Partner: The First Lady in the Twentieth Century* (Westport, CT: Greenwood Press, 1991), p. 51; Carl Sferrazza Anthony, *First Ladies: The Saga of the President's Wives and Their Power*, 1789-1961 (New York: William Morrow, 1990), p. 439; Betty Boyd Caroli, *First Ladies* (New York: Oxford University Press, 1986), p. 184.

3. "Mrs. Hoover Talks Over Wide Hookup," *New York Times*, April 19, 1929.
4. Arthur Hyde to LHH, May 20, 1929, June 5, 1929 and LHH to Hyde, May 21, 1929, "Radio Talk to 4-H Members," AAS, SF.
5. *Idem.*
6. The first two broadcasts are discussed in the *New York Times*, March 24 and May 7, 1931. The text of the November 7 speech is in *Idem.* For the arrangements for the May 6, 1931 meeting, see Mrs. Kermit Roosevelt to Mildred Hall, April 16, 1931, Kermit Roosevelt Papers, Box 54, Manuscripts Division, Library of Congress.
7. *New York Times*, November 6 and November 7, 1931.
8. "The Woman's Place in the National Emergency, November 27, 1932," AAS, SF.
9. Gutin, *The President's Partner*, p. 49; *New York Times*, September 27, 1932.
10. *New York Times*, November 22, 1930 and October 8, 1932 (last two quotations).
11. The background of the DePriest episode is covered well in David S. Day, "Herbert Hoover and Racial Politics: The DePriest Incident," *Journal of Negro History* 65 (Winter 1980), pp. 6–17; Donald J. Lisio, *Hoover, Blacks and Lily-Whites: A Study of Southern Strategies* (Chapel Hill: University of North Carolina Press, 1985), pp. 135–140.
12. Mary Randolph to Mr. Rockwell, June 5, 1929 (two messages), list of names marked Tea, Wed., June 12, 1929, also lists for teas on June 4, 1929 in "1299 Events," White House Social File series, LHHP. DePriest is quoted in *Journal of the Senate of Texas Being the Second Called Session of the Forty-first Legislature, 1929* (Austin, Tex.: A.C. Baldwin & Sons, 1929), p. 195.
13. Diary entry for June 8, 1929, Ruth Fesler Lippman Papers, HHPL; Lisio, *Hoover, Blacks and Lily Whites*, pp. 135–136.
14. Unsigned note, DePriest, June 1929, in DePriest Incident, SF; *Journal of the Senate of Texas*, p. 195; Oscar B. Colquitt to Dan Moody, June 20, 1929, Oscar B. Colquitt Papers, Box 2E1733, Center for American History, University of Texas at Austin. Colquitt's letter was an effort by one of the Hoover administration's supporters to explain that the invitation was not "A personal act of the First Lady of the Land."
15. Mary Austin to LHH, June 21, 1929; Lewis A. Lincoln to LHH, June 20, 1929; Elizabeth B. Talbert to LHH, June 20, 1929 in DePriest Incident: Approving Mrs. Hoover's Actions, SF.

16. Mary Elizabeth Alison to LHH, June 15, 1929; H. C. Jennings to LHH, June 15, 1929, DePriest Incident: Approving Mrs. Hoover's Actions, SF. The White House clerks missed the sarcasm of Taylor's wire.

17. Herbert Hoover, *The Memoirs of Herbert Hoover: The Cabinet and the Presidency* (New York: Macmillan Company, 1952), p. 324; Presidential Appointments Calendar, HHPL; Pryor, *Lou Henry Hoover*, p. 181.

18. LHH to Genevieve Brady, April 14, 1930, April 25, 1930, May 2, 1930 (quotation), GSAC, POA; Frances D. McMullein, "Girl Scouts Continue to Win New Members," *New York Times*, September 30, 1928; "Mrs. Rippin is Dead; Girl Scout Leader," *New York Times*, June 3, 1953.

19. LHH to Genevieve Brady, August 14, 1930, GSAC, POA. For information on Gilbreth, see Edna Yost, *Frank and Lillian Gilbreth: Partners for Life* (New Brunswick, N.J.: Rutgers University Press, 1949) which does not mention Lou Hoover, and Ruth Schwartz Cowan, "Lillian Evelyn Moller Gilbreth," in Barbara Sicherman and Carol Hurd Green, eds., *Notable American Women: The Modern Period* (Cambridge, Mass.: Harvard University Press, 1980), pp. 271–273.

20. Lillian M. Gilbreth to LHH, May 18, 1930, June 20, 1930, September 15, 1930, GSAC, POA. The organization of the President's Emergency Committee for Employment is discussed in Albert U. Romasco, *The Poverty of Abundance: Hoover, the Nation and the Depression* (New York: Oxford University Press, 1965), pp. 143–144 and Martin L. Fausold, *The Presidency of Herbert Hoover* (Lawrence, Kansas: University of Kansas, 1985), p. 99.

21. Genevieve Brady to LHH, January 28, 1931, GSAC, POA.

22. Alice M. Dickson to Ruth Fesler, GSAC, POA; Arthur Woods to LHH, March 25, 1931, LHH to Woods, March 31, 1931, text of radio address, March 23, 1931, AAS, SF.

23. *New York Times*, May 7, 1931, September 1, 1931.

24. Sara Louise Arnold to LHH, September 21, 1931, GSAC, POA; Birdsale Otis Edey to LHH, September 10, 1931, GSAC, POA. Mrs. Hoover discussed the work of the Rapidan meeting in the speech she gave to the Girl Scout Convention. See Girl Scout convention address, October 14, 1931, AAS, SF. For the term "Rapidan Plan," see *New York Times*, October 16, 1931, and *Washington Post*, October 16, 1931.

25. LHH to Mrs. Frederick Edey, October 16, 1931, GSAC, POA. *New York Times*, October 16, 1931.

26. "Mrs. Hoover Urges Living Normal Life," *Washington Post*, October 15, 1931; Lillian M. Gilbreth to LHH, October 19, 1931, November 19, 1931, December 10, 1931 and undated letter, all in GSAC, POA.
27. Radio Broadcast to 4-H Clubs, November 7, 1931, AAS, SF.
28. Girls Scout convention speech, October 7, 1932, AAS, SF; "Mrs. Hoover Lauds Girl Scout Relief," *New York Times*, October 8, 1932.
29. "The Woman's Place in the National Emergency," November 27, 1932, AAS, SF.

Chapter 5: Lou Henry Hoover and the White House

1. Interview with Lillian Rogers Parks conducted by the author in Washington, D.C. in July 1982. Similar views were expressed by other members of the White House staff in interviews conducted for the Herbert Hoover Oral History Program.
2. Ava Long, "Presidents at Home," *Ladies Home Journal* (September 1933): 80
3. LHH to her children and grandchildren, July 1932, Allan Hoover Papers, HHPL.

Chapter 6: First Lady in the Arts

1. Oral history interview with Hulda Hoover McLean, HHOP, pp. 13–14.
2. LHH to Mrs. Baldwin, August 14, 1937, Friends of Music, POA.
3. LHH essay "The Independent Girl," School Papers: High School Reports and Miscellaneous, SF.
4. LHH to Edgar Rickard, November 17, 1932, White House: Music, SF.
5. Tibbett as quoted in the *New York Times*, April 20, 1929.
6. Glen Plaskin, *Horowitz: A Biography* (New York: William Morrow, 1983), p. 142.
7. Mildred Dilling to LHH, February 27, 1933, PC.
8. Robert Russa Moton to Herbert Hoover, March 13, 1930, White House, The: Artists Who Wish to Appear—Hampton, Presidential Subject File, HHPL.
9. Notes concerning a telephone conversation, December 9, 1932, *Ibid.*
10. Ruth Fesler to LHH, February 24, 1930, Social Events at the White House: Mr. Junge—Musicales, WHGF.

11. Wallace E. Moody, "Chief Yowlache, Civic Symphony, Feature at Park" (unidentified clippings, probably San Diego, California), *Ibid.*
12. Oral history interview with Sue Dyer, HHOP, p. 65.
13. LHH to Elizabeth Sprague Coolidge, July 14, 1936, PC.
14. LHH to Mrs. Baldwin, August 14, 1937, Friends of Music: Correspondence, POA.
15. "Friends of the Community," *Daily Palo Alto Times*, August 15, 1940, Friends of Music, POA.

Chapter 7: Carrying On: Lou Henry Hoover as a Former First Lady

1. Speech by LHH, "The Woman's Place in the Present Emergency," November 27, 1932, broadcast nationwide by NBC, AAS, SF.
2. LHH to Allan Hoover, January 31, 1933, Allan Hoover Papers, Hoover Presidential Library (hereafter AHP).
3. LHH to Allan Hoover, February 11, 1933, AHP.
4. Oral history interview with Lillian Rogers Parks, HHOP, page 39.
5. LHH to Allan Hoover, April 8, 1933, AHP.
6. LHH to Allan Hoover, May 17, 1933, AHP.
7. *Idem.*
8. Oral history interview with Helen Pryor, HHOP, pp. 3–4, 11–12. Mrs. Hoover's interest in Stanford students was mentioned by many oral history interviewees, notably Grace Bowman, Philippi Harding Butler, Mildred Hall Campbell, Thomas Allen Campbell, Marie McSpadden Sands, and Helen Green White.
9. LHH to Allan Hoover, October 22, 1933, AHP.
10. *Idem.*
11. Talk by Lou Henry Hoover, February 24, 1936 over radio station KGO, San Francisco, transcript in AAS, SF.
12. Pryor, *Lou Henry Hoover*, p. 220.
13. Oral history interview with Hulda Hoover McLean, HHOP, p. 23.
14. Tribute by Dare Stark McMullin for the *Girl Scout Book of Memories* (1944) in Hoover, Lou Henry: Death and Funeral-Memorials and Tributes: Girl Scout Book of Memories, SF.
15. LHH to Herbert Hoover, April 21, 1937, AHP.
16. LHH to Herbert Hoover, September 13, 1937, AHP.
17. LHH to Herbert Hoover, November 23, 1937, AHP.
18. LHH to Sue Dyer, March 28, 1938, "Pro America," POA.
19. Herbert Hoover to LHH, August 10, 1938, AHP.

20. Herbert Hoover to LHH, February 9, 1939, AHP.
21. LHH to Mary Pickford, December 17, 1940, "Salvation Army: Clothing Drive of 1940," POA.
22. Herbert Hoover to LHH, November 30, 1940, AHP.
23. LHH as quoted in, "Lou Henry Hoover: A Tribute from the Girl Scouts," p. 5, Hoover, Lou Henry: Death and Funeral—Memorials and Tributes: Girl Scouts, SF.
24. Oral history interview with Edward Anthony, HHOP, p. 53.
25. *Idem.*
26. Oral history interview with Hulda Hoover McLean, HHOP, p. 40.
27. Will of Lou Henry Hoover, November 17, 1943, Margaret Hoover Brigham Papers, HHPL.
28. LHH to Irene H. Gerlinger, February 16, 1942, Hoover, Herbert: Biographical Comments by LHH, SF.
29. *Idem.*
30. This was a practice of several years' standing. See Servants and Aides: Thompson, Leon and Agnes, SF.
31. Oral history interview with Margaret Rickard Hoyt, HHOP, appendix.

Chapter 8: *The Documentary Legacy of Lou Henry Hoover*

1. LHH to Jackson Reynolds, November 24, 1914, PC.
2. LHH to her children and grandchildren, July 1932, AHP.
3. LHH to David Starr Jordon, February 15, 1916, Hoover, Herbert: Presidential Enthusiasts, SF.
4. LHH address at Girl Scout conference, c. 1926 as quoted in Lou Henry Hoover: A Tribute from the Girl Scouts, Lou Henry Hoover: Death and Funeral—Memorials and Tributes: Girl Scouts, A Tribute from, SF.
5. *Idem.*

About the Contributors

JAN BERAN is a professor of sport history at Iowa State University, a former Fulbright professor in Nigeria and Taiwan, and a guest lecturer at three universities in the People's Republic of China. Her academic publications include articles on the history of Iowa women in sport, Lou Henry Hoover and athletics, and Iowa girls' basketball. She recently completed a book-length manuscript: *A Century of Iowa Girl's Basketball.*

During basketball's centennial in 1991, she trained a group of Iowa State University women to play basketball by the 1899 women's rules. Clad in old-fashioned middy blouses and bloomers, these players have been in demand for demonstrations across the Midwest and throughout the nation.

ROSEMARY F. CARROLL is an attorney and a professor of history at Coe College where she also chairs the History Department. Since she joined the Coe faculty in 1971 she has directed the Continuing Education Program for Women, the Truman Scholarship Program, and the American Studies Program. Other administrative duties include serving as an advisor to pre-law students and as the college's affirmative action officer. She has addressed the annual Hoover symposium at George Fox College in Newberg, Oregon, and is presently at work on a full-length biography of Lou Henry Hoover. Having completed most of her research on Lou's formative years, she has begun to acquaint herself with Mrs. Hoover's activities in the 1920s.

REBECCA CHRISTIAN is a graduate of the journalism school at Iowa State University. A successful freelance writer with several books

147

and many newspaper and magazine articles to her credit, she is also a commentator on KUNI radio (a National Public Radio affiliate in Cedar Falls, Iowa) and a columnist for the *Dubuque Telegraph-Herald*.

Christian is best known as the author of four plays including the highly regarded *First Lady Lou*, a one-woman show based on the life of Lou Henry Hoover. After an extensive tour sponsored by the Iowa Humanities Board, *First Lady Lou* traveled to the Smithsonian Institution and the National Archives in Washington.

LEWIS L. GOULD is Eugene C. Barker Centennial Professor of History at the University of Texas. Professor Gould is a member of the Board of Editors of *Presidential Studies Quarterly* and the author of a number of books on the Spanish American War, the progressive era in American politics and several in-depth studies of presidents William McKinley, Theodore Roosevelt and Woodrow Wilson.

Professor Gould's interest in first ladies began during his study of the three progressive era presidents and increased significantly during research for his book *Lady Bird Johnson and the Environment* which was published by the University Press of Kansas in 1988. His most recent book, a study of the election of 1968, was published in 1993 by Ivan R. Dee.

ELISE K. KIRK is an author, lecturer, musicologist, a university professor, piano soloist, and leader in the promotion of the performing arts. Her publications include more than forty articles, essays, and reviews in magazines and professional journals. In 1987, she received the Deems Taylor Award from the American Society of Composers, Authors, and Publishers for her book *Music at the White House* (1986). Her leadership as program director of the Dallas Opera's 1980 international symposium on "Opera and Vivaldi" received an award from the National Endowment for the Humanities and resulted in the publication of yet another book, *Opera and Vivaldi*.

She is currently editing an eight-book series on American music and finishing a book entitled *Opera—The American Experience*. Other recent projects included planning concerts for the Smithsonian's 1988 Stephen Foster Memorial and the White House Bicentennial Committee.

DALE C. MAYER is an archivist at the Hoover Presidential Library and has written and addressed groups across the country on a wide

148

variety of documentary preservation and archival management issues. After over twenty years' experience assisting researchers, he is equally at home with military history, domestic policy issues, foreign relations, and social history.

He was the project coordinator for the arrangement and description of the Lou Henry Hoover Papers prior to their opening for research in 1985-1986. His most recent publication, an appraisal of "The Quiet Leadership Style of Lou Henry Hoover," was written at the invitation of the *Presidential Studies Quarterly* for a special issue on first ladies.

WILLIAM SEALE is a highly regarded social historian and historical preservationist. His books include *The Tasteful Interlude* (1975); *The President's House* (2 vols., 1985); *The White House: The History of an American Idea* (1992); and *Of Houses and Time* (1992). His restoration projects include Travellers Rest in Nashville, Tennessee, and the George Eastman House in Rochester, New York, among many other historic houses, five governors' mansions, and seven state capitols. He resides in Alexandria, Virginia, and Jasper, Texas.

RICHARD NORTON SMITH is a 1975 graduate of Harvard University and is currently director of the Hoover Presidential Library. A former writer for the *Washington Post* and other publications, he began writing speeches for Massachusetts Senator Edward Brooke in 1977. Since then he has worked for Senator Bob Dole and has prepared speeches for Senator Pete Wilson, Vice-President and Mrs. Dan Quayle, and President Reagan.

His first major publication, *Thomas E. Dewey and His Times*, was one of three finalists for the 1983 Pulitzer Prize in biography. Subsequent volumes include *An Uncommon Man: The Triumph of Herbert Hoover* (1984); *The Harvard Century: The Making of a University to the Nation* (1986) and *Patriarch: George Washington and the New American Nation* (1993). Currently he is at work on the first full-scale biography of Col. Robert R. McCormick, the controversial publisher of the *Chicago Tribune*.

Index

151